Unlocking the Heart of the Artist

Matt Tommey

the**worship**studio

The Worship Studio
www.theworshipstudio.org

Title: Unlocking the Heart of the Artist
Author: Matt Tommey

ISBN-13: 978-1460930250
ISBN-10: 1460930258

Formatting by: Joshua Jack Consulting
joshuajack.com

Unless otherwise quoted, all Scripture quotations are from the Holy Bible, New King James Version, (NKJV). Copyright © 1982. Thomas Nelson, Inc.

Scripture quotations marked (NIV) are from the Holy Bible, New International Version. Copyright © 1973, 1978, 1984, International Bible Society.

Scripture quotations marked (NLT) are from the Holy Bible, New Living Translation. Copyright ©1996 by Tyndale House Publishers, Inc., Wheaton, IL 60189.

Scripture quotations marked (MSG) are from The Message. Copyright © 1993, 1994, 1995, 1996, 2000, 2001, 2001. Used by permission NavPress Publishing Group.

Scripture quotations marked (NASB) are from the New American Standard Bible. Copyright © 1960, 1962, 1963, 1968, 1971, 1972, 1973, 1975, 1977, 1995 by the Lockman Foundation. Used by permission.

Scripture quotations marked (KJV) are from the King James Version of the Bible.

Table of Contents

About the Author

Matt Tommey has been engaged in creative ministry for many years in both the US and internationally as a worship leader, songwriter, speaker and visual artist. He is the founder of The Worship Studio and serves as Pastor of Worship Arts at King of Glory Church in Asheville, NC.

Out of his own journey of brokenness, Matt has a deep passion to see artists and creative people walk in wholeness and reveal the Glory of God through their creative expression in ways that facilitate cultural transformation, economic revitalization and revival. Through mentoring, teaching, and his own creative expression, Matt is pursuing a life that reflects the Glory of God.

Matt is also an entrepreneur, basket maker and member of the Southern Highland Craft Guild. Married to Tanya, they live in Asheville, NC and have one son, Cameron. Matt regularly blogs on all things creative at WorshipMinistry.com and on his blogs for The Worship Studio.

Acknowledgements

Writing this book would not have been possible without the tireless efforts of my fellow artists at The Worship Studio, colleagues in ministry around the world and the ones who just plain love me. Specifically, I'd like to thank Lynn Rinehart, Ellen Bennett, Cathy Little, Bessie Watson Rhoades, Roy Rhoades and David Van Koevering for their unselfish contributions to this work. Tom Gill, my editor and friend, for his tireless efforts to make me sound great and communicate my heart. Patricia Reeves for opening the doors to the Downtown Mission Gallery in Canton, Georgia and seeing the vision of The Worship Studio when there was nothing but a dream in my heart and a word from the Lord. Tom Tanner and the folks at Riverstone Church for helping me to come out of the wilderness and embrace my calling. Jim & Pat Banks for the years of unconditional love, support, friendship and mentoring you have poured out on my family. Sam & Eliza Fine and the people of King of Glory Church in Asheville, NC for allowing me to pursue the dreams that are in my heart in the context of the local church and beyond. Ray Hughes and Dave Markee for being spiritual fathers and prophetic visionaries in my journey toward God's purposes in my life as a father to artists. The late Bob Cagle, who hired me to run the 'craft shack' at Camp Glisson during the summers I was in college. It changed my life.

My mother, Cheryl W. Crosby for declaring the Word of the Lord and the purposes of God in my life over me since I was in the womb. My son, Cameron for teaching me what it is to be a father, to love and to be loved.

Lastly, to my beautiful, incredible wife, Tanya. You inspire me. You make me laugh. I love being near you. You are God's perfect gift to me and I love you with all my heart!

Matt Tommey
Asheville, NC - December, 2010

What Others Are Saying. . .

"*Unlocking the Heart of the Artist* is a must read for those who have had their creativity blocked or dormant as well as those wanting to take the next step in advancing His Kingdom through their own creative expression. As one who leads prophetic art and creativity seminars, I will be encouraging my students to devour every morsel of this amazing book!"

Janice VanCronkhite
Nationally Acclaimed Artist and Speaker

"This is a remarkable book. If there is another even remotely similar, I have not seen it. It speaks to a largely untouched area in our society and represents the happy and significant fact that God has left no venue in our world without a witness of His cosmic plan, His Eternal Kingdom. Thanks Matt for your strange and remarkable "hobby", for your wonderful understanding of the whole, big story of God and human redemption and, most of all, for you willingness to put it in print for all of us."

Jack Taylor
Author, Christian Leader & President of Dimensions Ministries

"I enjoyed reading Matt Tommey's book very much. It was a joyful and humbling experience; humbling because many of the ideas and principles within are accurate reflections of my own thoughts regarding the artistic development of the church. Joyful because it goes further than my own in terms of its potential to spur on the raising up of schools and fellowships of artists in the future. The practical teaching section towards the end of the book is especially worth study.

"The Body of Christ is in desperate need of people who are gifted in prophetic administration, and it would seem that in Matt, we have someone whom God could use mightily in this area. I heartily recommend Matt's book to all who are looking to improve their skills as artists, and to those who desire a deeper understanding of the power of creativity and those who are called to serve the Church in this way."

Dave Markee
Speaker, Musician & Author, *The Lost Glory*

"Matt nails it! This is not just a book. It's a manual for a new generation of kingdom artists. Matt's writing is honest, vulnerable and prophetic. If you want to grow your influence as an artist, read this book."

Mark Nysewander
Teaching Pastor, RiverStone Church

"Matt Tommey knows what makes us artists tick—our motivations, our fears, our aspirations, our sin natures, even our inner dialogue. In short, Matt knows the heart of the artist. And in his book, *Unlocking the Heart of the Artist*, Matt gives us the tools and the insight to grow in the fullness of Christ that is intended for us as artists.

"Grounded firmly in Scriptural truth, Unlocking the Heart begins with the calling and lineage of the Christian artist, moves through the issues of self-deception, self-worth and acceptance, and into finding one's unique voice and calling of our creative expression. Through it all, he gives a practical yet personal view of God's heart. And in the process, he encourages us to find ourselves—creative and complete—in the inspiration of God."

Manuel Luz
Creative Arts Pastor, Songwriter, and author of *Imagine That: Discovering Your Unique Role as a Christian Artist*

"I can honestly say this work is extraordinary. It is the most articulate work I have read that reveals a comprehensive Biblical basis for artists to unashamedly pursue their powerful gift and calling, and when brought under the power of the Holy Spirit that gift can have a dramatic redemptive influence in lives and culture. It's *The Purpose Driven Life* for artists. It reads with ease and the workbook format makes its implementation all the more doable.

"Masterpiece Christian Fine Arts has witnessed the very thing of which you speak as we have traveled with the 'Let There Be Light' exhibit in major cities in the last three years, bringing redemption for the lost and new hope for the Believer. I would encourage every artist who desires to be a vessel most "useful to the Master" to read your book. Well done!"

Jeanne Randall
President, Masterpiece Christian Fine Arts Foundation

"*Unlocking the Heart of the Artist* is to release within the creative self, the ability to receive and hear the whisper of God's intent for your creativity. We 'creative spirits' must come to consciously know we are who we are. I am me, but I am not mine. . . You are who you are, but you are not yours. . . My gifts are not mine. Your potentials are not yours. Only as we comprehend that all creativity flows through our spirit from the gentle Holy Spirit who leads us into all truth and is the only Source to show us creative things to come. We represent His creativity. Our art is not ours - It is only His.

"This book is a step - a huge step toward a godly lifestyle. These concepts are so carefully yet powerfully prepared. My life as an artist had missing, for most of my life, what is so simply and clearly stated here. Oh, if I had had these teachings earlier, how my values and potentials would have been so much more effective.

"The youth of our world now have these insights and will receive the Holy Spirit's data dumps and reveal His power through their art and shall cause all forms of creativity to establish His Kingdom on the earth as it is in Heaven."

David Van Koevering
Writer, Speaker, Inventor & President, Elsewhen Research

"*Unlocking the Heart of the Artist* is a practical, detailed, and well rounded book which will help any artist find his Divine purpose and inspire them to excellence and joyful fulfillment. This book is pleasantly grounded with scripture. Matt Tommey did a unique job at connecting artistry with God's mission and His kingdom work in the earth. Most books on music and artists take a secular, non-kingdom, view that is wrapped up in the culture of business and western-ism. Congratulations to Matt for this book that is a must read for those in creative arts."

LaMar Boschman
Author, Bible Teacher & Director of LaMarBoschman.com

"Written with the heart of a modern-day Asaph, *Unlocking the Heart of the Artist* beautifully displays the insight our Father has given Matt to the unique heart of the artist. Matt provides pivotal keys to unlocking the doors many artists have kept closed and hidden; many of which hold creativity not yet tapped into. An excitement will be stirred in your spirit as you learn from Matt's personal journey. It makes you want to go deeper - to get close to God, hear His voice, and dream with Him, so you can prophecy through creativity and advance God's Kingdom."

Christie Wilson
Worship Pastor, Christian Heritage Church

"As a church planter focusing on reaching creatives for Christ, I'm constantly looking for high quality resources that will help us disciple our community of artists. Unlocking the Heart of the Artist is a great tool for us! Matt Tommey has captured the essence of what we struggle with as creative Christ followers. Thank you Matt!"

Kerry Jackson
Lead Church Planter, Bezalel Church

"Wonderfully written, deep, thoughtful, challenging. This book will help you unlock your creative calling in ways you never thought possible. Matt Tommey is possibly the best Worship Leader you have yet gotten to know! You will be moved by this book!"

Gary Miller
Founder, WorshipMinistry.com

"With *Unlocking the Heart of the Artist*, author Matt Tommey offers artists of all types a map for a journey that some may not even realize they need to take; a journey that leads to a destination that none of them would not want to miss. It is a must-read for any creative type who desires to realize his or her full creative potential."

Cathy Little
Worship Leader, Author & Founder, Simply-Worship.org

"Matt Tommey has written a powerful book that will impact and stir the hearts of creatives of all types. In a disarmingly transparent style, Matt weaves his own story and lessons learned along the way into a solid biblical look at the calling of artists in the Kingdom. This book is a must read for those involved in leading creative arts ministries. The thoughtful discussion questions included with each chapter make it a natural choice for a small group format. I believe *Unlocking the Heart of the Artist* is part of a sovereign move of God to raise up musicians, painters, dancers, etc. to be a prophetic voice to the world."

Diane Thiel
Songwriter & Worship Pastor, Marietta Vineyard Church

"In *Unlocking the Heart of the Artist*, Matt takes us on an exhilarating journey in pursuit of wholeness and a renewed vision for artists of faith. I believe his desire for communities of artists to be established for spirit, soul and craft development is inspired by the Holy Spirit, and a key to the coming New Renaissance in the arts."

J. Scott McElroy
Founder, The New Renaissance Rising Arts Renewal Movement
and Author, *Finding Divine Inspiration*

"After Israel left Egypt, God unlocked the hearts of two artists, Bezalel and Oholiab, and then instructed Moses to entrust them with the design and construction of the Tabernacle. Today, God has unlocked the hearts of countless artists and has instructed Matt Tommey to sound His clarion call: '*Artist. Be loosed into your creative calling in God's Kingdom!*'

"As an artist himself, Matt has a keen understanding of the woundedness of most creative people. This book not only highlights the call of God on His creative ones, but also dispenses a healing balm that is vital in order for artists to operate effectively in His Kingdom."

Sam Fine, Senior Pastor
King of Glory Christian Church, Swannanoa, North Carolina

"I have known Matt for a long time. We first met when he was a student at The University of Georgia where I was a campus minister. I knew the first time I heard him play and sing that Matt had a special talent. His voice and his passion really had the ability to capture a room. Even as a twenty-year-old college student, he stood out. That was almost twenty years ago. The thing I have really come to appreciate most about Matt Tommey as I have gotten to know him is his heart. It's not his heart for music or even his heart for worship that makes him special. It's his heart for Jesus. Matt is desperate for the presence of our God. And the Lord has gifted him with a special ability to take others with him into that special place.

"In Unlocking the Heart of the Artist Matt articulates clearly that all who want to make this journey are invited. Thank you Matt for a much needed glimpse into the heart of the artist. Keep dreaming! The best is yet to come."

Tom Tanner
Lead Pastor, Riverstone Church, Kennesaw, GA

"I am so pleased to endorse both this book and its author. As an inner healer for 20+ years it warms my heart to find those who are vitally interested in healing the hearts of artists. As a group, artists are perhaps the greatest communicators of our time, and consequently among the most influential of our age.

"Unfortunately, it is because of the gifts they carry and that potential influence they are capable of in every element of society that the enemy has targeted them for some of the worst abuse imaginable. That abuse was not targeted at their ability, but their individual identity. It is our personal identity that determines what we do with our gifting, ability and talents. I am so grateful that someone has chosen to provide a resource assisting in that healing effort from a Godly perspective as a means of allowing the deposit of the glory of God in each of them to be fully revealed."

Jim Banks
Founder/Director, House of Healing Ministries

"Matt's new book is an admirable call to artists to submit their creative lives to the Triune Creator who alone can unlock creative hearts. The Author and Finisher of our Faith desires full abandonment to His Word and His powerful Spirit. Matt encourages artists to glorify God in their work and be instruments to reveal His Kingdom. Thank you, Matt, for sharing your creative journey."

G. Carol Bomer
Internationally Acclaimed Painter

Foreword

God created us in His image. We have been created, by the creator, to be creative. He also created us to be worshippers. So, if we are not worshippers of our creator, we forfeit the reason or purpose for us to exist . . . a simple reality that is often overlooked. Sadly, this is one of the reasons why some of history's most gifted and creative people lived such tortured lives. Ever seeking and never finding is a sad lyric, to say the least. Yet, that has been the song of many a dreamer with a locked heart. Truth be told, there are probably more Christians struggling with locked heart issues than non-Christians. I cite religious rules, unrealistic restrictions, and fear of man as the dominant violators of the born again heart. However, the stories behind locked hearts can be as diverse and unique and as creative as the individuals that tell them. And it's not always that complicated or poetic.

It can be as simple as life's situations and circumstances that ruthlessly rob you of the luster needed to live beyond your next crisis. For some, busy schedules are said to be the formidable and unconquerable enemies of our creativity and worship. Most of us are so busy with life that we cease to fully live. How many lyrics have been lost to the clamor and clatter of busyness? How tragic, to think of how many wondrously creative loved ones from past generations seemed to have lost their time to lives half lived. So many never had or took the time to fully live the greatest passions of their hearts. Sadly for many of us, too much living-time is spent existing and surviving. Unfortunately, true creativity and authentic worship are given backseats when surviving and existing becomes our focus. People who are caught in that web are usually heartbroken, or at least severely disappointed or shutdown.

Life simply has too many unforgettable moments that are too often forgotten... A worshipper has too many moments in God's presence that are also too often not fully lived. I believe, among other things, that "worship happens when you sense an acute awareness of the presence of God, and God senses an acute awareness of the presence of you." Because those moments are so precious, they should be fully lived. Those moments should be songs, poems and works of art. They should be dances, sculptures, paintings, carvings, pottery, etc. By bringing our creativity into the atmosphere of worship to our creator, we have the ability to expand the atmosphere and extend or magnify our worship.

God made you and me to be a "one of a kind" unique and memorable or "remember-able" creative creation. So, our creativity is a way that He has given us to capture those moments of worship and sustain them as a reminder or a memory to acknowledge that He is a "one of a kind" true, awesome, eternal, timeless, wondrous God.

Undoubtedly Matt has been a given a special gift and grace to help us all walk through the unlocking process. His insight and revelation is a vital key to a prophetic generation of culture shaping, creative worshippers.

Ray Hughes

Speaker, Musician & Author, *Sound of Heaven, Symphony of Earth*

Founder, Selah Ministries

Introduction

"The Glory of God is Man Fully Alive" – St. Irenaeus

As one of the Father's creative ones and one who has spent a lifetime trying to figure out what that meant, this book is for me as much as anyone. This journey is about unlocking your heart, connecting you with the Father and teaching you to engage the Holy Spirit in your creative expression. It is also an attempt to facilitate the release of your heart as you fully engage in all that God has for you within the context of His Kingdom.

Over the years, I have encountered many artists, musicians, craftsmen and other creative ones who have, for one reason or another, become stuck. The 'stuckness' originates from many different places – woundedness, fear, control, unbelief, religious barriers – and creates a frustration in their life that becomes unbearable. Many artists, unable to understand what is really going on either run headlong into 'creativity for creativities sake' or turn to unhealthy alternatives in order to numb or overcome the pain they are feeling. Many more simply give up, hide the gift by stuffing it down under 'Christian work ethic' and just try to gone on with life as usual.

Whatever your flavor of 'stuckness', the Father wants you to be fully released to worship Him through your creative expression. His desire is that nothing holds you back from creative destiny for your life – not even yourself. This journey is about embracing the divine calling for your life as an artist in the Kingdom, getting in touch with your unique prophetic voice and releasing it in a way that not only effects culture, but the heavens. It is also about you being fulfilled and happy! The Father's desire for your life is not that you just be productive or even that you work for Him – it is that you live a life fully engaged in His presence; a joyful, passionate and creative life where you are enjoying Him as much as He enjoys you!

I want to encourage you – do not just make this a quick read. It is designed to be chewed on, discussed, mulled over and digested. And when you are done, come back to it again and again as a source of inspiration and focus. The Father cannot wait for you to see how He sees you and to release the secrets of His Kingdom into your heart. It is time for His creative ones to walk in the destiny and fullness that He's designed for you. Your heart beating fast, your imagination vivid, your eyes wide with wonder and desire – that is His desire for you! A life fully alive, fully engaged, fully embracing the creative destiny He's given you. All that He has created you to be colliding with the Source of all creativity – that is what you are about to experience. He has been waiting for this moment your whole life. Get ready – your destiny awaits!

Tools for the Journey

As we begin this journey together, I want to put "5 smooth stones" in your bag, so to speak. These are simply tools that I believe the Lord has breathed on to help illuminate His voice to you during this season of your life.

Journaling

Taking time every day to center yourself in the Lord and really get in touch with your heart and His voice is crucial for your journey as an artist in the Kingdom. Every day, your assignment is to begin writing random thoughts, prayers, conversations, ideas – just write. As you begin to 'uncork' your heart, you'll be amazed at what the Lord begins to show you. Don't go back and read the entries just yet. Just write.

Creative Space

A weekly 'date' with your creative self. This is time where you pull away to feed your heart – to engage in activities that draw out creativity from your life. Sometimes it's as simple as going to an art supply warehouse and browsing, visiting a museum, having an extended time of 'studio time', watching a great movie, etc. Don't skimp on this! You'll be surprised when and where the Lord begins speaking to you!

Soaking Worship & Prayer

Every day, take time to engage the Lord in what we like to call "soaking". Turn on some of your favorite worship music or instrumental music and lay in the floor, on a couch or somewhere comfortable. Breathe deeply and ask the Lord to meet with you, to speak to your heart, so soak you with His presence. It may be uncomfortable at first, but you'll learn to run to this as a haven of rest and creativity. This is a great time to listen for the voice of the Father, journal your thoughts and be with the One who is the Source of All Creativity!

Reading God's Word

During your times of soaking prayer and worship, I encourage you to spend significant time in God's Word – the Bible. While the Holy Spirit can speak to and lead us in many different ways, I find His voice particularly prominent when I am allowing the 'water of the Word' to flow over me in His presence. The Bible teaches that Jesus is the Word (John 1:14) – the more you expand your appetite for the Word, the more revelation and understanding you will receive about Jesus, the Kingdom and His purposes for your life and art. Ask the Holy Spirit for direction and devour the Word as your source of life and sustenance. The Father longs to share the mysteries of His Glory as you explore the depths of His Truth.

Community

I encourage you, as much as possible, to not take this journey alone. There are things on this journey that can't be experienced in a vacuum. We were created for community! Share your journey with others who share your passion for creativity and connecting the Father! Some people have taken the book and done it as a study group, reading a chapter a week and discussing it over coffee or at a friend's house. Ask the Lord for creative ideas.

Chapter 1
Your Calling as an Artist in the Kingdom

It has taken most of my adult life to really get in touch with who God has called me to be in His Kingdom. Most of that time has been spent, not in trying to figure out what God wants, but in figuring out who I am and what I was created for. Something powerful happened inside my heart and my very spirit when I started to get it – I mean really get who it was I had been created to be. The point of convergence in my life came after many years of struggle, confusion, and years of trying to achieve the results of a life I thought I wanted. I'll be sharing my story with you throughout this journey of "unlocking the heart of the artist."

So the real questions for each of us become, "Who am I?" and "What have I been created for?" If you get nothing else out of this book, these two questions must be answered in order for your life as an artist to have meaning, passion and fulfillment in Christ. Until then, like many frustrated artists you will run headlong after stuff you think you want or a life you thought you were meant to live only to discover that the real you was left somewhere in the distant past.

What Makes You Unique?

As an artist in the Kingdom, and more importantly a child of God, it is vital that you realize you were created for greatness in the image of your Father! The spirit of excellence, power and healing that resides in His very DNA resides in you. The very creativity that dreamed and formed everything you know as life today is your inheritance in Christ. Through your salvation in Him, you now have a new DNA that has been downloaded into the core of who you are.

To an artist, that can seem kind of bland – everybody getting the same thing every time a 'new creature' is born. However, the exact opposite is true. To be created in the image of God is to reflect the unique depth and beauty of His heart. Our Father is the source of all creativity, the source of all life, the source of all beauty and passion. He is like a diamond with endless facets to be explored; like a galaxy that is ever expanding with no end, depth, height or length. As His artists, each one of us is endowed with a unique expression of His heart and able to reflect His beauty in the earth. The Glory that resides in Him resides in you through Christ Jesus, and through the power of the Holy Spirit the Father wants to release Glory through your creative expression.

You may tend to struggle with the concept of your own greatness, your unique power in the Kingdom or even with your role as an artist. This chapter is designed to help you explore your own uniqueness in the Kingdom of God as an artist – a carrier of His Glory – and to discover the prophetic voice He has called you to be.

What Burns in Your Heart?

The calling of God on our life, and our unique expression of that call, is many times reflected in the things that we are naturally passionate about. For example, one of my passions has always been music – singing, writing and playing piano. Even as a child, no one ever had to make me practice, or sing, or get involved in music; it just came naturally. I soon realized that God had gifted me in that area and as I began to explore it further, I realized that my natural talents were giving me clues about God's calling on my life. The same was true with Appalachian folk art and crafts. I have been a basket maker now for about 15 years, but that passion began to appear in my life as a teenager who loved being outdoors, making things with my hands and being creative.

What burns in your heart? Is it music or songwriting? Are you a painter or sculptor? Does writing creative stories or working on a stained glass piece really get your internal motor running? At the end of this chapter are some questions to help get you moving. Take a moment to explore what it is that you're passionate about. Write your answers in your personal journal.

What Were You Created For?

This may seem like a loaded question, but at the end of the day you have a calling and a future in God that is just for you and ordained by Him! As you walk this journey of unlocking you will begin to see that future become more and more clear. Although everyone has a unique calling in the Kingdom, there are some foundational elements to those called as artists.

Relationship with the Father

You were created to be in relationship with the Father through the person of Jesus Christ and empowered by the Holy Spirit, not to merely fulfill some dead, dry religious obligation or to keep a bunch of rules that don't fan the flame of passion in your life. The Bible implies in Genesis 3 that Adam and Eve walked with the Father in 'the cool of the day' as a part of their daily relationship. Throughout the gospels, Jesus told the 'religious people' that they will not inherit the kingdom because 'He never knew them.' The more you are with Him the more you become like Him and begin to dream His dreams for your life. You begin to see His vision for the future of your generation.

Co-laboring in the Kingdom

You were created to co-labor with Christ in the Kingdom of God through your unique creative expression. God has promised the secrets of the Kingdom as your inheritance (Luke 8:10). That means God has ideas, strategies and insight into situations you are passionate about and He wants to reveal those strategies to you in order to see His Kingdom established in the earth. He has chosen to use you to do the works of the Kingdom in power in your generation.

Show Forth His Glory

You were created to reflect, reveal and release the Glory of God in the earth through your art. Bezalel, a master artist, was chosen by God to represent His Glory to Israel and others through the building of the Tabernacle of Moses:

> *"See, I have called by name Bezalel the son of Uri, the son of Hur, of the tribe of Judah. And I have filled him with the Spirit of God, in wisdom, in understanding, in knowledge, and in all manner of workmanship, to design artistic works, to work in gold, in silver, in bronze, in cutting jewels for setting, in carving wood, and to work in all manner of workmanship."* - Exodus 31:2-5

The Bible describes the work of Huram (a skillful artist) in Solomon's temple in detail. Based on the account, Huram was *"filled with wisdom and understanding and skill in working with all kinds of bronze work. . ."* (1 Kings 7:13-45).

To War in the Heavenlies

You are called to war in the heavenlies through prophetic acts of worship and artistic displays inspired by the Holy Spirit. Worship and praise of God in any form, not just music, inflicts judgment on the enemy:

"Let the high praises of God be in their mouth, And a two-edged sword in their hand,
To execute vengeance on the nations, And punishments on the peoples;
To bind their kings with chains, And their nobles with fetters of iron;
To execute on them the written judgment—This honor have all His saints.
Praise the Lord!" - Psalms 149:6-9

Your worship may be music or it may be another form of divinely inspired creative expression. Whatever it is, it is considered an attack on the enemy because it carries the Light of the presence of God. When the Light of His presence goes forth into the atmosphere, it pierces the darkness, proclaims victory to the captive, heals the sick, binds up the brokenhearted and proclaims the year of the Lord!

Your Personal Artist Statement

Now that you are beginning to understand some of the foundational elements to your calling in the Kingdom, I want to encourage you to write your own personal artist statement. This statement is unique to you and should describe your specific calling and future in the Kingdom as you currently understand it. Ask the Lord for revelation about how He wants to use you to show forth His Glory in the earth. Then go for it! Use your own personal journal as the canvas for this new creative work!

Journaling and Discussion Questions:

1. *"What makes you unique?" Ask the Lord for insight into how He uniquely created you.*

2. *God says He will give us the desires of our heart when we delight ourselves in Him (Psalm 37:4). What are the desires of your heart?*

3. *In terms of creative expression, what are your natural gifts and talents?*

4. *When you move in those gifts and talents, how do you feel?*

5. *Do you sense God's pleasure in those activities? Have you ever seen Him use you to touch others while doing one of those things?*

6. *What do you do every day, week, month to cultivate your gifts?*

7. *Write about a time when you were affirmed because of your creativity, artistic expression or uniqueness.*

Chapter 2
Your Spiritual Lineage as an Artist in the Kingdom

Beginning a journey like this one is exciting! This may be the first time in your life that you ever considered your calling as an artist in the Kingdom. On the other hand, you may be walking closely with the Father and be an artist who is going to the next level in God. Wherever you may find yourself in this journey, it is important to start from the same place.

Consider these questions...
✓ Who are you?
✓ From whom have you come?
✓ Where are you going?
✓ What obstacles may be lying in your path?

Part of navigating this journey together comes through understanding where we get our identity as artists. Some people say we are born with it, others say it is developed. I think it is a little of both.

At the end of the day, whether you are a master artist or are emerging in your calling, an experienced craftsman or just a person with a creative bent looking for more, all artists share the same spiritual lineage. It is foundational therefore to understand where you get your spiritual and creative identity – from your natural state or from the source of all life and creativity – and that you have the ability, like most things in the Kingdom, to choose!

Where you choose to secure your identity sets the course for your life and experience. There is a tendency, especially for artists and creative people, to just "go with the flow" and do what feels "natural." But if your heart and mind are not redeemed you can quickly be led astray.

Where Is Your Heart?

The prophet Jeremiah said, *"The heart is hopelessly dark and deceitful, a puzzle that no one can figure out."* (Jeremiah 17:9 MSG). Proverbs 3:5-6 (MSG) reminds us to:

> *"Trust God from the bottom of your heart; don't try to figure out everything on your own. Listen for God's voice in everything you do, everywhere you go; he's the one who will keep you on track."*

I mention these 2 Scriptures up front because they shine a light on our tendency to do what comes naturally. The dangerous part is that what comes naturally, especially to artists, can lead down some crazy roads. Take for example, the story of Cain and Able in Genesis 4:

> *"Adam lay with his wife Eve, and she became pregnant and gave birth to Cain. She said, 'With the help of the LORD I have brought forth a man.' Later she gave birth to his brother Abel.*
>
> *"Now Abel kept flocks, and Cain worked the soil. In the course of time <u>Cain brought some of the fruits of the soil as an offering to the LORD</u>. But Abel brought fat portions from some of the firstborn of his flock. The LORD looked with favor on Abel and his offering, <u>but on Cain and his</u>*

offering he did not look with favor. So Cain was very angry, and his face was downcast.

"Then the LORD said to Cain, 'Why are you angry? Why is your face downcast? If you do what is right, will you not be accepted? But if you do not do what is right, sin is crouching at your door; it desires to have you, but you must master it.'

"Now Cain said to his brother Abel, 'Let's go out to the field.' And while they were in the field, Cain attacked his brother Abel and killed him.

"Then the LORD said to Cain, 'Where is your brother Abel?'

"'I don't know,' he replied. 'Am I my brother's keeper?'

"The LORD said, 'What have you done? Listen! Your brother's blood cries out to me from the ground. Now you are under a curse and driven from the ground, which opened its mouth to receive your brother's blood from your hand. When you work the ground, it will no longer yield its crops for you. You will be a restless wanderer on the earth.'

"Cain said to the LORD, 'My punishment is more than I can bear. Today you are driving me from the land, and I will be hidden from your presence; I will be a restless wanderer on the earth, and whoever finds me will kill me.'

"But the LORD said to him, 'Not so; if anyone kills Cain, he will suffer vengeance seven times over.' Then the LORD put a mark on Cain so that no one who found him would kill him. So Cain went out from the LORD's presence and lived in the land of Nod, east of Eden." - Genesis 4:1-16 (NIV; emphasis added)

First of all, you may be asking "Why are we talking about Cain and Abel?" Well, if you skip ahead in the story to verses 17-25, you'll realize that Cain is the great, great, great grandfather of all the artists and creative ones. We'll explore this relationship more in a moment, but for right now let's look at some of the attributes of Cain's life.

Attributes of Cain's Life

1. **First-Born**: From all accounts, it seems he had some major control and ego issues with his brother, Abel and with God.
2. **Farmer**: He worked with his hands to produce a harvest from the natural environment.
3. **Brought an Unacceptable Offering**: he brought the fruit of his work (farming) to the Lord and made an unacceptable offering, after the Lord had evidently set standards for him of what was acceptable and unacceptable.
4. **Got Angry and Sinned**: Since God accepted the offering of His brother, Abel, and not his, Cain allowed jealousy and rejection to get hold of his heart, causing Him to sin by killing Abel.
5. **Banished**: Because of Cain's sin, the Father banished Cain from His presence, the source of all life.
6. **No Fruit**: Banishment from God's presence caused barrenness in Cain's life. No matter how hard he worked his fields would no longer produce.
7. **Homeless**: Once gone from God's presence, Cain became a homeless fugitive, constantly wandering.
8. **Unsettled**: When Cain finally settled, it was in the land of Nod, which means "wandering." The rest of his life was spent in a place of unsettled homelessness.

It is very interesting that the attributes of Cain's life almost mirror the lives of many artists and creative people. The reason is because Cain is the natural father of all creative people. In our unredeemed state, without a life-giving relationship with the

Father, through Jesus, we look just like Cain. Let's break it down a little further with some attributes that may describe your life or the experience of other artists you know.

Attributes of the Old Identity

1. Ego and Control Issues
2. Mistrust of Authority
3. Desire to worship the work of our very own hands (see Isaiah 2:8)
4. Jealousy and Rejection Issues
5. Feelings of Shame and Fear
6. The "Starving Artist" Syndrome – the harder you work, the less you get
7. A Wandering, Restless spirit

Just because that's your natural lineage, doesn't mean you can't come into a new life in the Kingdom and have Christ redeem and restore your creative DNA. God has always been about redemption; He loves to take what is broken down and discarded and breathe His life into it. In fact, as you'll see in this story, He loves to go out of His way to see His purposes established in the earth!

Restoration Generation

Five generations after Cain, in the generation of grace (5 is the number of grace in the Bible), God began a work of redemption in the lives of the artists to restore us to Himself. In that generation the Father restored double with two descendents in Cain's lineage. Their names are Jubal and Tubal-Cain. As musicians, artists, craftsmen and creative ones, these guys are two of our spiritual fathers.

"His brother's name was Jubal. He was the father of all those who play the harp and flute. And as for Zillah, she

also bore Tubal-Cain, an instructor of every craftsman in bronze and iron..." - Genesis 4:21-22

Our Father went out of His way to restore the line of the creative ones bringing a double portion blessing where there was only jealousy, rage and death. He did this because He loves us and has called us according to His purposes in our generation and beyond!

As we continue to look at our lineage in the Kingdom, the Father gives us a vivid picture in the story of Bezalel and Oholiab of what a healthy artist really looks like when they are restored and walking in the fullness of their calling. The story begins with Moses calling out to the people of Israel, saying, *"All who are gifted artists among you shall come and make all that the Lord has commanded"* (Exodus 35:10).

Moses went on to describe everything that was to be made for the Tabernacle including the work of sculptors, metal artists, embroiderers, seamstresses, jewelers, tanners, woodworkers, silversmiths, spinners and the like. (Being a basketmaker, I'm sure Moses just forgot to mention us!)

Moses then called out Bezalel and Oholiab from all the craftsmen of Israel saying:

"Then Moses said to the Israelites, 'See, the LORD has chosen Bezalel son of Uri, the son of Hur, of the tribe of Judah, and he has filled him with the Spirit of God, with skill, ability and knowledge in all kinds of crafts – to make artistic designs for work in gold, silver and bronze, to cut and set stones, to work in wood and to engage in all kinds of artistic craftsmanship. And he has given both him and Oholiab son of Ahisamach, of the tribe of Dan, the ability to teach others. He has filled them with skill to do all kinds of work as craftsmen, designers, embroiderers in blue, purple and scarlet yarn and fine linen, and weavers--all of

them master craftsmen and designers.'" - Exodus 35:30-35 (NIV)

Out of the tribe of Judah (meaning 'praise'), God called a craftsman with a father's heart to show forth His Glory in the earth through the building of the Tabernacle of Moses. Some of the attributes of Bezalel and Oholiab were:

- **Chosen:** Their calling sets them apart from the crowd. They were the best of the best in their creative pursuits.
- **Worshippers:** Bezalel was from the tribe of Judah. Worship was at the core of His heart and DNA as an artist.
- **Filled and Skilled:** They were "filled with the Spirit of God with great skill, ability and knowledge in all kinds of crafts." These men were the picture of renaissance artists, able to balance the pursuit and practice of their skill within the context of the anointing. When God begins to rise up in you, your gifting will be expanded and multiplied!
- **Prophetic:** By making the furnishings for the Tabernacle of Moses, God was using them to create artistic works of great prophetic significance in their generation and beyond. Their work also hosted the power and presence of God, transmitting His presence to the people of their generation.
- **Fathering:** Bezalel and Oholiab were both men with hearts to teach and raise up others in their calling. Though not often seen, it is a beautiful picture of artists selflessly giving themselves to others to build them up and see them reach the fullness of their artistic pursuit!

The Tabernacle of David

We see the same kind of healthy, spiritual lineage in the Tabernacle of David with Asaph, Jeduthan and Heman – three more of our spiritual fathers. These men were a threefold cord of anointed leadership that God used in their generation to raise up future generations of worshippers, musicians and prophets.

> *"David, together with the commanders of the army, set apart some of the sons of Asaph, Heman and Jeduthun for the ministry of prophesying, accompanied by harps, lyres and cymbals"*

> *"All these men were under the supervision of their fathers for the music of the temple of the LORD, with cymbals, lyres and harps, for the ministry at the house of God. Asaph, Jeduthun and Heman were under the supervision of the king. Along with their relatives--all of them trained and skilled in music for the LORD--they numbered 288. Young and old alike, teacher as well as student, cast lots for their duties."* - 1 Chronicles 25:1; 6-8 (NIV)

Again, you see anointed artists – spiritual fathers – under Godly authority (David); raising up other artists to play skillfully and prophetically. Remember, Bezalel was filled and skilled as well.

These musicians were also *"under the direction of their fathers as they made music in the house of the Lord."* You see, Godly order values experience and skill, while never discounting the verve and passion of the younger generation. The hearts of these spiritual fathers were turned to their children in the spirit of Malachi 4:6, and God radically blessed the unity in their midst by making the Tabernacle of David a place of His unparalleled habitation for years and years.

NOTE: I believe two of the reasons music and arts are so divisive in the church today are: 1) the lack of Godly order in the ranks of the musicians and artists – no spiritual fathers and mothers, and 2) many churches hire personality and style over anointing and skill to please culture or look "cool." This creates a recipe for division and disaster in a local body.

Stepping Into Your New Identity

You see my friend, the Father wants to bring you out of the false, unredeemed identity of brokenness, shame, fear, control, rejection and jealousy into the fullness of His DNA for your life and creativity in Christ! His heart is that you are filled with the Spirit of Wisdom and Revelation in the knowledge of Him (Ephesians 1:17) so that the eyes of your understanding are opened to His Glory. He desires you to operate under His grace as a wise, skillful, anointed artist who reflects and releases His Glory in the earth.

As an artist, you have a rich calling in God, but you have to make a choice. From whom will you receive your lineage; Cain or Christ? Even though there may be patterns engrained in you from the old identity, God has already realigned your spiritual DNA in Christ so that everything Christ has, you have. Now it is up to you to receive His finished work and allow God to break your old patterns and establish new ones.

In the next chapter, you'll learn a little bit more about my story and how to overcome the spiritual roadblocks in your own life. God wants to see you healed, whole and restored so that everywhere you place your foot – everywhere you place your work – you take the Kingdom! Right now, I'd like to invite you to do a little self-inventory.

Journaling and Discussion Questions:

1. *How do you respond to God's radical display of grace and restoration toward you after Cain's sin?*

2. *What does it mean to be "filled and skilled?"*

3. *What is the fruit of your life? Your art?*

4. *Are you struggling with the same things Cain struggled with?*

5. *Are you enjoying frustration or fruitful creativity?*

6. *Are you raising up others around you or are you fearful of being found lacking?*

Chapter 3
Roadblocks to Your Creative Expression

As a creative person with a calling in artistic expression, my ability to feel and sense things has always been a major part of my life. That is the way God designed all of us – to sense and respond to His Spirit in order to flow with Him in the Kingdom. For most of my life, this ability to sense and feel deeply was a double-edged sword because of areas of deep woundedness in my own life. Instead of operating out of a healthy place, sensing the Spirit of God and His flow, I was ruled by negative emotions – shame, fear, guilt, control – until it paralyzed my ability to function. Shut down by this storm of emotions, I created an "alter-ego" that everyone loved (performance was the name of the game) but was unable to maintain for long.

My life continued to roll along in this performance-oriented posture until over a period of a few months it all came crashing down around me. On the outside, I was this perfect guy – talented, happy, creative, successful – everything that seemed "too good to be true." In reality, I was a hurt young boy on the inside, fighting for my life with the only tools I had ever learned; secrecy, addiction and control. Slowly, my creative ability and intuition was withering away to nothing. I used to be energetic, focused and able to sense the anointing as I led others in worship, now I just faked it and performed. Very few knew the difference, but inside I was dying. The grace to continue under these contrived circumstances was quickly evaporating.

Steal, Kill & Destroy

See, the enemy loves to take the very thing that God has gifted us with and turn it around on us in order to kill us. The Bible is very clear that the enemy seeks nothing else but to steal from, kill and destroy everything that we are.

> *"A thief is only there to steal and kill and destroy. I came so they can have real and eternal life, more and better life than they ever dreamed of." -* John 10:10 (MSG)

If the enemy can attack you at your core and win, then he has destroyed the very essence of who you were created to be. Look at King David, for example. A man described by God as "after His own heart" – full of passion, desire and love, yet because of the unhealed places in His heart the enemy was able to twist his heart and redirect His focus into lust, war, control and performance.

From all accounts David, as a boy, was a loner who grew up on the backside of a sheep pasture by himself. Through the stories we know of his life it is obvious that his relationship with His brothers and his father was probably not the best. Was his dad even proud of him? When the prophet, Samuel, came to choose the new king, David's dad didn't even think to include him in the lineup.

As I look at David's life, I see a young boy with a distant father, brothers who didn't think much of him, tremendous artistic gifting and yet not a lot of affirmation. Like many artists, David's need to be accepted, affirmed and fathered was left lacking. The result was a creative man with a calling and lots of vision but whose passions took him in another direction. Instead of turning to the Father for wholeness and affirmation he turned to lust, greed and another man's wife. It wasn't until David went through a major period of brokenness and repentance in His life that he really got on track with all that God had for him. After he was able to get real with his "stuff" and walk through some healing he saw the greatest creative inspiration of His life come forth, the building of what we know today as The Tabernacle of David and fathering generations of creative worshippers.

God's Plan for Restoration

The Father's design for you is the same as it was for David; that you are healed, restored, fulfilled and uninhibited in order to reflect His Glory through your life and creative expression. The Greek word for this process is "sozo" which means to be *saved, healed and delivered*. That process begins when you accept Jesus into your heart, continues when you are baptized with His Holy Spirit and matures as you walk with the Father daily in relationship with Him and His Body. The Father's desire is that you walk in wholeness in such a way that deep wounds are healed, strongholds are broken, truth is revealed, and old "doors" formerly accessed by the enemy in your life are closed. The brutal truth for most artists and creative people is that the process of wholeness is not an easy road.

Beauty

In our western culture beauty can be just a product of Photoshop, a vanishing vapor of our imaginations created by the media moguls' intent to sell us their products or services. Yet truthfully, beauty is the very essence of God. Scripture says *"Honor and majesty surround him; strength and beauty are in his dwelling"* (1 Chronicles 16:27 NLT). Psalm 50:2 reminds us that God is the perfection of beauty, saying *"From Mount Zion, the perfection of beauty, God shines in glorious radiance"* (NLT). Our Father, God of all Creation, the ONLY uncreated one IS beauty. So why is it so easy for us to get sidetracked into going down paths that promise everything but leave us empty and wanting more?

Like David's life, ours is often consumed with the pursuit of beauty. As God's creative ones we are wired to desire beauty. We are attracted to it, seek it out and want to surround ourselves with its very essence. Since we are wired for beauty, the enemy creates mirages that seem to be exactly what we are looking for. The reality however, is that they lead us to places we never intended to go and then leave us stuck on the muddy road of heartbreak and frustration, cowering behind emotional and spiritual roadblocks. The enemy's promise of fulfillment is the same old lie from the tree of good and evil in the Garden – "God doesn't really know what is best for you; come over here where the grass is greener and find what you are really looking for." This is called deception and it is what the enemy does best. Outside of the beauty of God and the Glory of His transforming presence we find only fleeting fulfillment and empty promises.

Roadblocks

In the Garden we were beautiful, our environment was beautiful and we freely enjoyed the beauty of the Father in the cool of the day. Everything was perfect. Sadly, when sin entered the picture through our own human weakness and the deception of an enemy who is out to kill us, we lost the ability to fully perceive the beauty of God. We quickly became satisfied with a myriad of counterfeits presented to us by the world in direct opposition to the purposes of God for our life. The initial roadblock is selfishness which opens the door for lack of trust. Adam and Eve believed, as we often do today, that they really could do this thing called life on their own; that God was trying to limit them and that if they wanted the real gusto in life and creativity, they had to go after it themselves.

The Bible says of Adam and Eve, *"The man and his wife were both naked and they both felt no shame"* (Genesis 2:25). What a wonderful picture – man and woman, fully loved, fully accepted and fully accepting of who they were in relationship to the Father. Just a few verses later though, the Bible says, *"Then the eyes of both of them were opened, and they realized they were naked; so they sewed fig leaves together and made coverings for themselves"* (Genesis 3:7). Because of their sin and selfishness, and their desire to go beyond what God had designed for them, and because they believed the lie of the enemy that the grass would be greener, they hid from God. Their shame produced what it always produces, fear. Fear then produced insecurity, which led to anxiety and stress. Anxiety produced an inability to trust and thus a forced posture of self-sufficiency.

Anytime we, like Adam and Eve, consider ourselves self-sufficient we separate our hearts from the Father. Separation then produces loneliness and more fear, compounding the cycle of destruction and separation into what I call "roadblocks." Instead of breaking through these roadblocks, many artists erect high and holy idols on and around these "sacred cows" protecting and coddling them at any cost. Their roadblocks become monuments to be revered instead of barriers to be destroyed.

How many artists do you know who have gone down the path of seeking ultimate beauty, truth and meaning in their art, only to be left holding the proverbial bag. As a result of their emptiness, anger and hurt other means of coping are developed (addictions to work, sex, alcohol, drugs, etc.) and they go into overdrive just to maintain the appearance that everything is OK.

I did this in my own life. As I mentioned previously, the grace to continue my double life was quickly evaporating. My sacred cow was the public persona I created and I would go to any and all lengths to make sure that nothing tarnished that image. I was perfect, there was nothing wrong and everything was just wonderful. At least that was the story. When anyone attacked my cow, either intentionally or unintentionally, the wrath of Matt was unveiled and there was a major price to pay. As a polite southern boy, I would always inflict my judgment through manipulation, never anger, and then mask all my feelings of inadequacy within the dark rooms of my addiction.

The temperament of artists is primarily feeling/sensing. As an artist, you may have had some major hurts and wounds in your life (as have many of us) so if you feel yourself shutting down or not hitting on all cylinders creatively, guess what? There is a connection! The enemy has crafted specifically for you the roadblocks that you are experiencing. The good news is that God wants you healed, restored, and happy so you can experience His fullness in this life. Jesus said He came so that we would have life abundantly, not just some dead, trudging up the mountain existence! Restoration is in the work of Christ and our Father is all about transformation. As you are intentional in your desire for the beauty of His presence, the roadblocks you now face will become your pathway to healing and unlimited creativity.

In the next chapter, you will discover how to identify and overcome the strategic roadblocks the enemy has laid in your path. These roadblocks are a bunch of lies, false beliefs and deceiving emotions that amount to a huge pile of garbage in your life. It is time to take out the garbage and prepare your heart to experience the beauty of God in all His fullness.

Journaling and Discussion Questions

1. *How do you respond to the story of King David at the beginning of the chapter? Does it sound familiar?*

2. *What are some of the roadblocks in your own life?*

3. *How have these roadblocks affected your life, relationships and creative expression?*

Chapter 4

Take Out the Garbage

During my own journey toward wholeness and restoration, I have discovered (stumbled onto) several keys that helped me walk through the roadblocks and into the destiny that God has for my life and creative expression. I'd like to explore these with you in this chapter, not as some "blueprint for success," but to offer glimpses into wholeness through the eyes of another artist. More than anything I want to help build your faith to believe that you don't have to live blocked-in and stuck any longer than you choose.

Previously, I described these roadblocks as garbage that stink up your creative flow and block your ability to experience the fullness God has for you. Anytime garbage and trash gets into your pipeline, it affects everything that flows through you. Imagine that your life is a clean pipeline designed to flow fresh, clear water through it. Now imagine a yucky buildup on the inside – trash, garbage, dirt, grime, oil, greasy residue. No matter how clean the water is that flows into the pipe, once it passes through that dirty conduit, it will come out dirty. There is no way around it.

That is how it is with your life and creative expression. God's intention is to pour life-giving water and refreshment through you, but when garbage is in the pipeline, it severely affects your ability to experience Him in all His goodness. As a result, your view of God becomes skewed based on the specific garbage you have in your life and thus it becomes a roadblock. The longer you allow these roadblocks to remain intact the larger they become and the more difficult they are to remove.

Stinkin' Thinkin'

You may have heard the phrase "stinkin' thinkin'". The truth of that phrase is that your thinking can cause a stink in your life if you are not careful – junk in, junk out.

I have discovered in my own life that most of the garbage I dealt with started with a belief about God or a situation that wasn't true. It goes like this: Something negative happens and because of my inability to understand or process the situation I develop a belief or judgment that is simply untrue. Compounding that are my words, beliefs and judgments that begin to create the reality that I experience, both positive and negative. *"For as he thinks in his heart, so is he"* (Proverbs 23:7a).

When I was a young teenager, my relationship with my father was really rough. So rough, that I began to subconsciously believe that all men in authority were bad, out to get me, and only wanted me to perform the role of the perfect son in order to be accepted. As I grew older, the fruit of those beliefs began to manifest in relationships with the senior pastors that I worked for. Suddenly, when they would critique me for a seemingly insignificant issue in my life or work, all the anger and rage I felt toward my dad would come to the surface. Subconsciously I would shut-down emotionally and withdraw my heart from them, and then work to sabotage the relationship through manipulation and control. This horribly destructive pattern played out in my life simply because of false beliefs and judgments that were formed as a 13 year old boy. It took me 20 years of relationship blowouts and lost jobs to figure out what God's truth was. Even though I was "anointed" and "called" to ministry my character had to be formed into the image of Christ. I had to experience the transformative power of His healing presence, not just sing about it. It was a long journey, but well worth the pain I endured to see healing manifest in my life.

To begin taking out the garbage in your life you must first examine what the "stinkin' thinkin'" is and correct it with what God says about you.

- What do you really believe about yourself?
- When you are all alone and life has slowed down enough for you to hear your own heartbeat, whose voice do you hear?
- Are you happy with who you are?
- Do you compare yourself to others who sing better, paint better, draw better, play better, or receive more accolades than you do?

Many artists call this the voice of the inner critic...that negative, attacking voice that rises up inside of you when you least expect it, knocks you back down to size and keeps you inside the box. It is the voice that says "You will never make it." or "Your work isn't up to par." or "Who would really want to see that?"

This voice is straight from the pit of hell and is that of the enemy that Jesus identified as the father of lies (John 8:44). He creates customized lies and plants them in your mind to feed on your own insecurity and woundedness. The only way to overcome these lies is with truth – the truth of God's Word!

Listed below are some common lies artists have believed about their relationships and artistic expression. From 0% to 100% estimate the percentage to which you live by each of these beliefs:

____% I must meet high standards of perfection to feel good about myself.

Examples: I'm not good enough. I don't have enough talent to sell my work. I came in third place in the photography contest; I'll never be as good as Sally.

____% I must have the approval of certain people (boss, friends, clients, patrons, parents) to approve of myself. Without their approval, I cannot feel good about myself.

Examples: The audience gave _____ a standing ovation. I never get that. Why did they buy Roger's painting; mine won't ever sell. My voice isn't good enough to sing with _____; they will never invite me to sing with them.

____% Those who fail (including myself) are unworthy of love and therefore should be blamed and condemned.

Examples: I couldn't sell a single painting; John will never love a loser like me. It's all my fault the art show was a failure. I didn't promote the concert enough and I caused the whole band to hate me.

____% I am what I am. I cannot change. I am hopeless. In other words, I am the sum total of all my past successes and failures, and I'll never be significantly different.

Examples: I will never overcome stage fright. My writing won't ever be good enough – I am a loser. I'll always be an addict and won't ever be able to support myself and my family – I suck.

Silencing the Inner Critic

Now that you have exposed the lies of the enemy in your own mind, it is time to learn how to silence the voice of the inner critic by comparing those lies to the truth of God's Word. At a conference recently, I heard a prominent Christian leader say: *"I can't afford to have thoughts in my head that are not in God's."* And neither can you. Ask Holy Spirit to...

- bring light into your situation
- reveal why these beliefs are holding you back
- replace false beliefs with His truth

Have you ever asked God what he says about you? The more His truth is established in you, the less of an opportunity the enemy has to gain a foothold in your belief system. The Bible says in Romans 12:2 *"And do not be conformed to this world, but be transformed by the renewing of your mind, that you may prove what is that good and acceptable and perfect will of God."* You can't do things like you have always done them and expect different results. If you want to see real Holy Spirit transformation in your life, you have to change your thinking. You must begin to believe and internalize what the Father says about you!

Take just a second and read some of these verses from God's Word. This is the truth that will set you free from the lies of the enemy.

- **You Can Do Anything**

    "'If you can'? said Jesus. 'Everything is possible for him who believes'" - Mark 9:23 (NIV)

    "Therefore I tell you, whatever you ask for in prayer, believe that you have received it, and it will be yours." - Mark 11:24 (NIV)

- **You have all You need**

  "And my God will meet all your needs according to his glorious riches in Christ Jesus." - Philippians 4:19 (NIV)

- **You have Abundance**

  "The thief comes only to steal and kill and destroy; I have come that they may have life, and have it to the full." John 10:10 (NIV)

- **You Don't Have to Be Afraid of Anything**

  "Have I not commanded you? Be strong and courageous. Do not be terrified; do not be discouraged, for the LORD your God will be with you wherever you go." - Joshua 1:9 (NIV)

- **You Will Be A Success**

  "Commit thy way unto the LORD; trust also in him; and he shall bring it to pass." - Psalm 37:5 (KJV)

- **You Are Complete**

  ". . . you have been given fullness in Christ, who is the head over every power and authority." - Colossians 2:10 (NIV)

- **You Are More Than A Conqueror**

  ". . . in all these things we overwhelmingly conquer through Him who loved us." - Romans 8:37 (NASB)

- **You Are Secure**

  "For I am convinced that neither death nor life, neither angels nor demons, neither the present nor the future, nor any powers, neither height nor depth, nor anything else in all creation, will be able to separate us from the love of God that is in Christ Jesus our Lord." - Romans 8:38-39 (NIV)

- **You Are Confident**

  "being confident of this, that he who began a good work in you will carry it on to completion until the day of Christ Jesus" - Philippians 1:6 (NIV)

- **You Are Free**

  "You have been set free from sin and have become slaves to righteousness." - Romans 6:18 (NIV)

- **You Are A Child of God**

  "Yet to all who received him, to those who believed in his name, he gave the right to become children of God." - John 1:12 (NIV)

- **You have Protection**

  "'Because he loves me,' says the LORD, 'I will rescue him; I will protect him, for he acknowledges my name. He will call upon me, and I will answer him; I will be with him in trouble, I will deliver him and honor him.'" - Psalm 91:14-16 (NIV)

Going Deeper

If woundedness or trauma has caused false beliefs to take hold in your life, deeper personal ministry or the help of a caring Christian friend, pastor or mentor may be necessary. Don't freak out about this. If you are like me you don't want to share your "stuff" with anyone, but trust me, and trust God. Real healing comes in the context of community – safe community – where you can share your faults and your junk, and take hold of the freedom that is yours in Christ. In fact, James 5:16 declares *"Make this your common practice: Confess your sins to each other and pray for each other so that you can live together whole and healed. The prayer of a person living right with God is something powerful to be reckoned with"* (MSG). Your healing is tied to healthy community and your willingness to get real with the people in your life that love you and love God.

Getting Free

Are you ready to break ties with these ungodly beliefs in your life? I hope by now that you can see how the war over your life begins and ends in your mind. If the enemy can get you to believe lies then he can get you to walk in lies and manifest lies in your life, and ultimately derail the purposes of God for you.

If you are ready to get free from the lies of the enemy then follow this roadmap to freedom. Right now where you are, pray the prayers listed below. As you do, take hold of the work that God does in your life and begin walking in victory. Then, in the future when Holy Spirit reveals false beliefs and negative patterns in your life, pray them again and if necessary, again and again until you are completely free and walking in the fullness of God's plan for your life.

Repent: "Father, forgive me for agreeing with the enemy and believing that I am _____." (fill in the blank with the lies you've believed)

Renounce: "I renounce and break all agreements I have made with the enemy that include _____ (list all that the Holy Spirit brings your mind). I am a child of the King and covered in His blood."

Rebuke: "I command the lie of unworthiness and _____ (fill in the blank) to leave my life, my mind and my soul in the Name of Jesus. I declare and decree its power over me is broken, in Jesus' name."

Receive: I receive you, Holy Spirit, in all your fullness and power in place of the lie that _____ held in my life. Fill my mind and my spirit with Your truth, peace, righteousness and love."

Replace: "I ask You, Holy Spirit, to establish truth in my inmost being in the place where the lie of the enemy once resided. I ask for peace and acceptance _____ (fill in the blank of what you want) to be incorporated into every part of my life."

Realign: "Father, realign me with Your purposes in the Kingdom for my life. Awaken the hope of Glory and the incredible future You have for me! Give me vision for what is to come and passion to see it come to pass! Your kingdom come, Your will be done in my life!"

As you break old patterns of thinking and establish the Word of God in your heart, your life will begin a dramatic shift into a Kingdom flow. Get ready! You will begin to see God show up in your life and your creative expression like never before! The pipes are clean, the road is cleared and the fresh water of Holy Spirit is now flowing, in Jesus' name!

Journaling and Discussion Questions

1. *What are some of the ungodly beliefs, thoughts and lies that have become a part of your normal thinking? Expose them here by bringing them into the light.*

2. *Do you struggle with the voice of the "inner critic?" What does that voice sound like?*

3. *Which Scripture verse stood out as the most applicable promise to your life right now?*

4. *What are some of the ways the Lord is showing you to "take out the garbage" in your own life?*

Chapter 5

Discover the Father's Heart for You

During my first two years of college, I attended a small Methodist junior college in the mountains of North Georgia. While there, I pledged a fraternity in order to pursue the manly image and macho thing I thought I needed to be a man. Doing so meant I had to endure a ridiculous and extremely rigorous "pledge period" over 6 weeks during winter quarter. At the end, if I made it through the gauntlet, I would be rewarded with full brotherhood and be established as a member of the fraternity.

In many ways my entire life had been like that. In order to receive the full inheritance and get the reward I had to be enough, do enough, say enough and perform well enough. Then, if I was found worthy, I had a chance of being accepted. Sadly, this same belief system carried over into my relationship with God. I treated Him like some egotistical dictator who needed to be entertained, so I would put on a show for Him singing, preaching and performing. Yet when I faced difficulties in my life or experienced failure, I ran away and hid so no one would know how bad I really was, especially God. I believed the lie that "if they really knew who I was, they wouldn't love me."

This could be the story for many artists, maybe even you. Living with the frustration of feeling like you never measured up, that your work was never quite good enough.

I remember this feeling as early as 12-13 years of age. I was a young boy, a musician, creative, energetic, talented and friendly. Of course, the other boys thought that I must be gay. Combine that with several years of sexual abuse by a same-sex family member and I was set up for a major identity crisis.

Even my relationship with my dad suffered. I felt as if nothing I did ever measured up to what he wanted. He was always on me for something I did or didn't do. After a while, I just became numb to the whole thing and began believing that nothing I did would ever be enough. Needless to say, I struggled with my own sense of identity for many years until coming to wholeness in Christ.

The Prodigal Son

At the end of our fraternity pledge period in college we were all given nicknames. Some guys were given names based on their "sexual prowess" while others were given names based on some trait or level of coolness. But my name was different...I was given the name, "Prodigal Son." That name stuck with me for a long time and in many ways, like most names, has defined my life – a wounded son who wanted his own way, believed the worst about his dad and wanted anything but to be where he was.

Let's look at the story of the Prodigal Son. As an artist, you may relate to it:

"Then he said, 'There was once a man who had two sons. The younger said to his father, "Father, I want right now what's coming to me."

"'So the father divided the property between them. It wasn't long before the younger son packed his bags and left for a distant country. There, undisciplined and dissipated, he wasted everything he had. After he had gone through all his money, there was a bad famine all through that country and he began to hurt. He signed on with a citizen there who assigned him to his fields to slop the pigs. He was so hungry he would have eaten the corncobs in the pig slop, but no one would give him any.

"'That brought him to his senses. He said, "All those farmhands working for my father sit down to three meals a day, and here I am starving to death. I'm going back to my father. I'll say to him, Father, I've sinned against God, I've sinned before you; I don't deserve to be called your son. Take me on as a hired hand." He got right up and went home to his father.

"'When he was still a long way off, his father saw him. His heart pounding, he ran out, embraced him, and kissed him. The son started his speech: "Father, I've sinned against God, I've sinned before you; I don't deserve to be called your son ever again."

"'But the father wasn't listening. He was calling to the servants, "Quick. Bring a clean set of clothes and dress him. Put the family ring on his finger and sandals on his feet. Then get a grain-fed heifer and roast it. We're going to feast! We're going to have a wonderful time! My son is here—given up for dead and now alive! Given up for lost and now found!" And they began to have a wonderful time.

"'All this time his older son was out in the field. When the day's work was done he came in. As he approached the *house, he heard the music and dancing. Calling over one of the houseboys, he asked what was going on. He told him, "Your brother came home. Your father has ordered a feast—barbecued beef!—because he has him home safe and sound."*

"'The older brother stalked off in an angry sulk and refused to join in. His father came out and tried to talk to him, but he wouldn't listen. The son said, "Look how many years I've stayed here serving you, never giving you one moment of grief, but have you ever thrown a party for me and my friends? Then this son of yours who has thrown away your money on whores shows up and you go all out with a feast!"

"'His father said, "Son, you don't understand. You're with me all the time, and everything that is mine is yours— but this is a wonderful time, and we had to celebrate. This brother of yours was dead, and he's alive! He was lost, and he's found!"'" - Luke 15:11-32 (MSG)

Awesome story, isn't it? This story causes me to weep almost every time I see it portrayed in film, music, or theatre because it is so close to home. That kid who knew it all, wanted to run and do his own thing. The one who found nothing but broken emptiness at the end of a long journey of self-indulgence was me. But who was this father? I mean really. For me this idea of a father who loved unconditionally and held no record of my rebellion was too good to be true. Honestly, about the only believable person in the story was that of the self-righteous older brother. Yet, this story is one of the most beautiful pictures that God has chosen to reveal Himself as Father to His children.

God's profound display of grace, mercy and love beyond reason is what makes the story so pivotal for us today. The story of the

Prodigal Son is especially poignant for artists because many of our stories look just like his, broken and tired, empty and wasted, longing to find the loving father we never believed existed.

Sadly, many artists have yet to come to know the loving embrace of a father who longs for them. That my friend is one of the key reasons I am writing this book – to help other artists like me, who are on the journey home wondering what lies at the end of the road.

Have you come to know His loving embrace? Understanding the Father's heart for you is key in your desire for home, your willingness to approach the Father and unlocking the treasure of creative expression inside of you. God is not looking for some stoic, religious exercise from you, neither does He want you just to roll over and become a robot. He wants all of you to receive all of Him in order to bless your socks off and impart abundant life to you beyond anything you thought possible! God wants to awaken His creative DNA within you and flow Spirit-led inspiration through your life like you have never imagined possible. He created you, knows you, loves you and accepts you where you are, how you are and who you are...no strings attached! You are God's child and through Jesus, He has made a way for you far beyond your wildest dreams.

With all of that in mind, let me share with you the Father who waits for you at the end of the road. This may not be the Father whom you imagined, but it is the Father that He is.

He Allows You to Walk Away

One of the most confusing things about the story of the Prodigal Son is that his father gave him the money in the first place. Had it been me, I would have been like "Dude! Get back to work!" I was comfortable with a father that controlled the situation at all cost and choreographed every move in order to suit his fancy and maintain his ultimate authority. Yet, in this story I see a Father who is not afraid of the choices I make.

Beginning in the Garden of Eden and throughout the Bible God's willingness to allow His children to choose something or someone other than Him is demonstrated. God is not worried. He is not scared. He knows that the only way you will ever really choose to love Him is if you have the ability to choose not to love Him. Only when you see and accept the emptiness of your ways will you truly realize the overwhelming goodness that the Father offers you.

He Loves You Unconditionally

The father in this story never stops loving and longing for his son to come home, just like our Heavenly Father. No matter what the son did while he was gone, or even what intentions he had when he left, the father never stopped loving him, just like our Father. His love went deeper than the son's ability to obey or disobey rules, just like the love of our Father. His love was an enduring love that knew no boundaries, just like the love of our Father. His was a love that kept looking, even when the son was running in the opposite direction, just like the love of our Father. We see in Jeremiah 31:2-6 (MSG) the same picture of this incredible faithful father who loves His kids even in the face of their turning.

"This is the way God put it:

'They found grace out in the desert, these people who survived the killing.

Israel, out looking for a place to rest, met God out looking for them!"

God told them, "I've never quit loving you and never will.

Expect love, love, and more love!

And so now I'll start over with you and build you up again, dear virgin Israel.

You'll resume your singing, grabbing tambourines and joining the dance. You'll go back to your old work of planting vineyards on the Samaritan hillsides,

And sit back and enjoy the fruit—oh, how you'll enjoy those harvests! The time's coming when watchmen will call out from the hilltops of Ephraim:

On your feet! Let's go to Zion, go to meet our God!'"

I love that! In verse 3, it says *"Israel, out looking for a place to rest, met God out looking for them!"* How incredible that our Father, in the midst of our searching for something other than Him, is still searching for and loving us without reservation!

That's my daddy!

That's *your* daddy!

He Accepts You In-Process

Not too long ago, I was at a men's retreat focused on recovery from sexual addiction. At the retreat, Sy Rogers, an incredible communicator on the subject of sexual brokenness, unpacked this whole idea of God's acceptance of "me in process" in a way that released tremendous freedom in my life. It was as if he turned on the light and said:

"Hey, listen! God created you! He knows your inmost being! He knows the beginning from the end and yet He chose to entrust His entire earthly ministry and the Kingdom to you – even though you are broken, messed up and in process. He's not nervous about you or the choices you've made! He knows right where you are and is walking with you every step of the way. He knew of your brokenness before you did yet He has not backed away from you one inch! In fact, He is waiting for you to get up and get back on the journey!"

If you are like I was, your view of God is all about Him requiring perfection and holiness in your life on a daily, minute-by-minute basis...no exceptions. Yet, the father of the prodigal son and the Father God we call "Abba" is not like that at all. He is one who:

✓ desires relationship with you through His son, Jesus
✓ requires obedience from you
✓ loves to forgive and restore so you can grow up and continue in the Kingdom

"For a righteous man falls seven times and rises again" (Proverbs 24:16). His acceptance of you is not based on your inability to hit the mark, but your willingness to get back up!

He Sees You through Eyes of Faith

Before Peter betrayed Him, Jesus said:

"Blessed are you, Simon son of Jonah, for this was not revealed to you by man, but by my Father in heaven. And I tell you that you are Peter, and on this rock I will build my church, and the gates of Hades will not overcome it. I will give you the keys of the kingdom of heaven; whatever you bind on earth will be bound in heaven, and whatever you loose on earth will be loosed in heaven." - Matthew 16:17-19

Even though Jesus knew Peter would publicly disown Him three times, He declared him strong, foundational and pivotal to Kingdom work in his generation. How is this possible? The loving father saw his prodigal son and Jesus saw Peter just as the Heavenly Father sees you today – through eyes of faith. God sees you right now in all the fullness and potential that He has placed within you. He is on the sidelines of Heaven cheering for you right now saying, *"I know you can do it! That's my boy! That's my girl! I'm proud of you! Keep going, you're gonna make it!"*

You may not believe that you have seeds of greatness in you, but the Father does. He knew you before you were formed in your mother's womb. He created you and put His DNA inside of you! He sees the extreme creativity and artistic expression He imparted to you flowing in fullness, affecting a generation and revealing His Glory to a hurt and dying world. Can you see it?

He Celebrates Your Desire for Him with Extravagance

When the father saw from a long way off his wayward son coming down the road, he ran to him and embraced him. Then his son began to confess his sin...

> *"But the father wasn't listening. He was calling to the servants, 'Quick. Bring a clean set of clothes and dress him. Put the family ring on his finger and sandals on his feet. Then get a grain-fed heifer and roast it. We're going to feast! We're going to have a wonderful time! My son is here—given up for dead and now alive! Given up for lost and now found!' And they began to have a wonderful time."* - Luke 15:22-24 (MSG)

The son was worried about what the Father would say. Would he accept him? Would he even recognize him? Would his father punish him for his disobedience and make him earn his status as a son? In direct contrast to the son's expectations, the father responded, not with simple forgiveness or even excited acceptance, but with ecstatic, abandoned extravagance. He stopped everything that was going on in order to celebrate the return of his lost son.

This is how the Father feels about you! Right now! No matter where you are on the journey home – not interested, just leaving or almost there – the Father is ready to pour out His extravagant love upon you! His kindness is what leads us to repentance (Romans 2:4).

He Defends and Protects You

As if showing his son extravagant acceptance was not enough, the loving father went one step further. He wanted his son to experience fullness of joy and life abundant so much that he not only celebrated the son's return, but defended him before his self-righteous brother in order to protect and cover his weakness.

It is the same with God. It is not about you just making it into heaven by the skin of your teeth. You have the same Father who desires to cover your weakness, build you up, celebrate your victories and love you in spite of your shortcomings. He wants you to experience fullness of joy and life abundant – here and now!

Just like the father in the story of the Prodigal Son, the Heavenly Father is looking for those who will simply turn their hearts to him. With a simple "yes" in his heart, the prodigal returned home to experience the fullness of his father's love.

Will you turn your heart toward Him? Will you dare to run to this Father who is even now looking for you? Beloved, He loves you!

Journal and Discussion Questions

1. *How do you respond to the father's unconditional love of the son in the story of The Prodigal Son?*

2. *Does your view of God as "Father" match up with the loving father in the story?*

3. *What are the core beliefs you hold about fathers and the Father? How have they affected your life and creative expression so far?*

4. *Now that you understand clearly who your Father is and how he feels about you, how does that change your perception of His plan for your life and creative expression?*

Chapter 6

Release the Dreamer: Co-labor with the Father in the Kingdom

Most of my Christian life as an artist has been filled with a fear of being too good, too performance-oriented or too prideful. In other words, I was taught that in order for me to be a Godly artist, I had to ride the humble train, passing through the towns of self-deprecation and abasement to really become all that God wanted me to become. I never understood that concept and could never find it in the Bible either. It seemed to me that the more God moved in a person, the more the desires of their heart were met, and as the desires of their heart were met, the more passionate they became. Honestly, I was confused and afraid to be passionate about my creative expression for fear of becoming labeled self-centered, prideful or arrogant.

The Bible teaches that Jesus came so that we might have life abundant (John 10:10b) and be passionate in every area, especially our creative expression. The things that we burn for in our lives and in our art are the very things God has birthed within us so that we can reflect His image.

Sadly, many artists have this man-inspired hang-up that God wants us to conform to some stiff, religious stereotype that ultimately cramps our style. I can't tell you the number of artists I've talked to who said that when they were growing up or when they became a Christian they felt pressured to be something they were not. And if the truth could be known, rather than try to be something we are not most of us would rather not be a part of that scene. Don't get me wrong. Jesus wants us conformed to His image in every area of our life, including our creative expression, but many of us have been sold a lie when it comes to what that actually looks like.

Fully Alive, Fully Engaged

When you look at the life of Jesus, you see the reality of someone fully engaged in life, solid in His identity and calling and yet totally focused and conformed to the image of His Father. He preached of life abundant (John 10:10) and at the same time said He only did what He saw the Father doing (John 5:19). For many artists there is a missed connection between total fulfillment, the uninhibited release of creative expression, and a life lived in total submission to the will of the Father. In fact, it is one of the most exciting truths in Scripture.

Understanding God's desire for you to be fully alive is key to your growth as an artist and as a believer. It frees you to be everything you are called to be with no fear, anxiety or worry about who you are or what your life looks like. Take a moment to read and respond to the following Scriptures in your journal:

- *"Delight yourself in the Lord and He will give you the desires of your heart."* - Psalm 37:4 (NIV)
- *"Praise the LORD! Happy are those who fear the LORD. Yes, happy are those who delight in doing what he commands."* - Psalms 112:1 (NLT)
- *"Jesus gave them this answer: 'I tell you the truth, the Son can do nothing by himself; he can do only what he sees his Father doing, because whatever the Father does the Son also does. For the Father loves the Son and shows him all he does. Yes, to*

your amazement he will show him even greater things than these.'" - John 5:19-20 (NIV)

Are you able to see that God wants you to be fully alive in Him, fully engaged in your passions and fully submitted to Him, and that your delight, your heart and your passions are rooted in Him? As you make that the posture of your life and creative flow, He will pour into you and through you what the Bible calls the "secrets of the Kingdom."

Releasing the Dreamer Inside of You

God is a dreamer. He dreams of:

- *A people who will love Him with all of their heart*
- *His Kingdom fully established on the earth*
- *His Glory poured out on all flesh*

The Word of God says these are His dreams, thus they become the dreams of His people as well.

God desires to strengthen you, to undergird you and to fan the flame burning inside of you as your heart becomes completely His. The Bible declares, *"For the eyes of the LORD range throughout the earth to strengthen those whose hearts are fully committed to him"* (2 Chronicles 16:9).

David was a dreamer who dreamed of the Glory of God being manifested in His generation. He also dreamed of a people worshiping the Lord before His throne in uninhibited freedom, and filled with great joy and adoration. Where did David's dream come from? Could it have come from the years David spent on the far side of a sheep pasture, worshiping the Lord and delighting himself in the love of the Father? It was during those times that David began to ask in his heart:

"What if...

...people could really experience the Father like I do, and not just some boring, religious ritual? What if God would come down and visit an entire nation like He comes and visits me when I worship alone in this field? What if God released creativity to whole teams of people to create instruments, write songs and minister to Him just like He has done for me?"

As David aligned himself with the heart of the Father, the Spirit of God began to rise up inside of Him and dreams were born.

Connecting to the Source

I have found in my own life that the closer I get to the heart of the Father, the deeper my passion grows and the bigger my dreams become. Not because I am some hotshot super-spiritual guy, but because I am intentionally connecting with the creative source of the entire universe – and He is my Father!

As artists, and sons and daughters of the Father, it is our DNA to be dreamers and to dream His dreams! Even in our humanness, our weakness and our frailty, when our hearts are inclined toward Him so that we begin to dream without inhibition, the Father releases secrets of His Kingdom into our hearts.

Once I began to experience this revelation in my life, everything changed – family, business, ministry and life in general. My outlook changed as well. I was no longer trying to become something I was never intended to be, a stove-up religious puppet trying hard to keep rules Jesus never intended for me. Instead, I was set free to pursue the heart of the Father and to dream big through the inspiration of the Holy Spirit.

The Secrets of the Kingdom are your Inheritance

Once you start dreaming and get outside of your religious, wounded, preconceived box, you will begin to see the bigger picture: You were created in the image of God to reflect His Glory in the earth, and in every area of life and creativity.

Every problem and every challenge that exists in the world today has a divine solution. God already knows about the problems we face and He has secret knowledge of how to fix them. For many people, the obvious question is: "Couldn't the Lord just solve these issues on His own?" The answer, of course, is "Yes. He is God." But the exciting thing about life in His Kingdom is that He gives that job to us! We are His hands on earth to accomplish His will as we are empowered and led by His Holy Spirit. He has called each of us to co-labor with Him in His Kingdom.

This is how it all happened for me: Dear friends of mine, Roy and Bessie, gave me a book by Bill Johnson entitled, "Dreaming with God" and strongly encouraged me to read it. They knew that I was in a season of searching and trying to hear from the Lord what was next for my life. Now I like to read, but this was one of those books that I could not put down. Very quickly I began to understand from Luke 8:10 that the secrets of the Kingdom are my inheritance.

I read stories Johnson wrote about people who just believed God and started dreaming outside the box, and how God showed up on the scene in a huge way. The more I read, the more my faith grew to the point that the day after I finished the book, I began to pray, *"Lord, I believe the secrets of your Kingdom ARE my inheritance. Lord, reveal to me secrets in your Kingdom!"* What happened next just blew me away.

I have been a basketmaker since 1993 and use primarily natural materials like kudzu vines, honeysuckle, wisteria, grapevine, poplar bark and the like. For those of you who may not know, kudzu is an Asian weed that is literally covering the south. It grows over a foot a day and blankets everything – trees, cars, houses, roads, slow moving cattle! Nevertheless, I have always loved that plant! In fact my father-in-law would say as we drove by a big kudzu patch "Boy, that's a lot of money." I would just laugh and shrug it off to southern humor.

When I began to pray for the secrets of the kingdom, however, the Lord spoke to me about kudzu of all things. I couldn't believe it. Who could love kudzu but Matt Tommey? I mean really, if I had a dime for every person that has ever said to me "Well I'm so glad someone has finally found something to do with that old kudzu!"

Without going into a lot of detail, Father told me in prayer and in a vision that kudzu was going to be used in a very strategic way in coming years. In addition, He gave me specific numbers, dates, formulas and other data to confirm His word to me. I started Googling around on the Internet and got some very clear prophetic confirmation – literally some of the things the Lord gave me were scientific data that was supposed to be secret and not released to the general public.

I was very excited that I was hearing the Lord, dreaming and beginning to see His hand at work in my dreams. I shared my vision with Roy and Bessie who said "You've got to share this with Dr. Chuck." So, I shared it with one of their friends, Dr. Chuck Thurston, a brilliant medical doctor and researcher. Upon hearing what I had received from the Lord he directed me to two friends of his that I needed to talk with, Ray Hughes and David Van Koevering. Ray Hughes had been a mentor to me from afar through his book "Sound of Heaven, Symphony of Earth" and "The Minstrel Series" powerful teachings for musicians. David Van Koevering just happened to be one of the leading researchers in quantum physics and worship.

I had already wanted to talk to Ray about The Worship Studio and everything we were doing in Atlanta to mentor artists, etc., but when I was introduced to him it was in regards to the kudzu dream I had. I thought "Thanks Chuck, but I need to talk to Ray about worship. This kudzu stuff can wait!" Little did I know, however, that days before I was introduced to Ray, he had given a prophetic word to a church in Clay County, Kentucky about the Lord releasing witty inventions to do with kudzu and how it was going to be used to bring economic empowerment to the area.

Ray was excited to meet me – he called me the "King of Kudzu" – so I drove up to Kentucky where he lived and met with him over lunch about what God had shown me. I still wanted to talk to him about The Worship Studio, but I decided to just be patient. When I told him about the vision he told me about two men that I had to meet, one was the pastor of the church where Ray gave the prophetic word about kudzu and the other was a "hillbilly preacher" up in eastern Kentucky with an invention that recycles garbage.

At the end of our conversation, I had just enough time to share with Ray about The Worship Studio. He loved the concept and said "Matt, you build it and I will come sit on the porch and teach them boys how to prophesy, just like Naioth Ramah." Ray is now on our board of advisors and a dear friend and mentor.

To make a long story short, through these prophetic connections, I am now a business partner with several Christian business men, researchers and engineers working to bring this God-given idea to fruition. The project is moving along very quickly because of how God has prepared the way before us with the government, businesses, and other organizations.

All of this happened because I dared to dream with God and believe His promise! Literally, we are standing at the door of impacting the world, advancing the Kingdom and generating millions of dollars in revenue because I chose to lie down on the floor, soak in God's presence and dream.

A Window to the Heart of God

Receive this into your heart right now! God has created you with a divine DNA, full of His creativity and power. He wants to pour through you in such magnificent ways that everything you put your hand to will usher in His Kingdom and release His Glory. Your art, your creative expression, is not just some hobby or mindless activity. Neither is it a waste of time that will never produce anything real. It is, in fact, a window to the heart of God designed for Him to flow His presence through in order to touch the lives of His people and change the earth.

As a creative person, you are especially sensitive to the world around you. By God's design, you feel and sense things that few others do. Just as God's Spirit is sensitive, so are you. It is part of what you reflect on the earth. As an artist, you have a specific medium in which you work, music, painting, fiber art, dance, movement, pottery, and the list goes on. Your creative "language" uniquely represents God's voice on the earth and in the Spirit.

Have you ever asked God what He wants to say through your art? What if you began to ask God for secrets of His Kingdom as it pertains to your creative expression? What if you began to dream God's dreams – big dreams; nation-changing dreams; economic-system-effecting dreams; healing dreams? Could God use your art, the creative expression of your hands, to bring healing? Could God give you an idea during your time with Him that could change a nation? Bring revival to a city? Release freedom to a person just by hearing a song you wrote or seeing a piece you just painted? Not only can He do this, it is the passion of His heart to release these dreams to you! Why? Because He loves you. God knows that when you passionately pursue Him in the Kingdom, you reflect His Glory and walk in your creative destiny.

The Father wants to release His Spirit upon you RIGHT NOW like on the day of Pentecost. He wants to give you a heavenly language that can communicate with people in a culturally relevant way, just like he did Peter! When that anointing begins to flow through you, the response of culture will be overwhelming! Look at what happened when Peter communicated the message of the Kingdom: *"When the people heard this, they were cut to the heart and said to Peter and the other apostles, 'Brothers, what shall we do?'"* (Acts 2:37). Likewise, hearts will be moved to respond as the power of God flows through your creative expression!

Your Sweet Spot

There is a sweet spot where God's Glory, your dreams, and reality all collide. Why is God glorified when you are in that sweet spot? It is because you are made in His image and He is very passionate, creative and loving. When you touch that part of Him through the expression of your life you reflect His Glory on the earth. Will you dare to live there? Will you dare to dream His dreams and co-labor with Him through your art?

Just a note as we end this chapter. Be careful who you share your dreams with... dream killers or flame fanners! We all need Jonathans beside us who will push us to believe in ourselves and the dreams God has birthed within our hearts! Ask the Lord to align you with people in the Kingdom who will encourage you and connect you with those who are strategically positioned to help make your dream a reality.

Journal and Discussion Questions

1. *How do you react when you hear that God's desire is for you to be fully alive and yet fully conformed to His image?*

2. *What does it mean to you to be conformed to His image as an artist?*

3. *What has God put in your heart? What are your dreams? Take a moment and without any inhibition, write down the dreams of your heart.*

4. *Take a moment right now and ask the Lord to enlarge your vision; your dreams of what is possible. Take your dreaming a step further, go way outside the box. Ask the Father what He wants to reveal to you and then write it down. Don't be afraid, it is probably much bigger than you think!*

Chapter 7

Develop Your Unique Prophetic Voice

"The spirit of prophecy is the testimony of Jesus." - Revelation 19:10

"Therefore, brethren, earnestly desire to prophesy..." - 1 Corinthians 14:39

"I would... that all prophesy..." - 1 Corinthians 13: 5

As one of God's creative people, you have been called to show forth the greatness and majesty of His name, just like the anointed Biblical artists who have gone before you. Bezalel and Oholiab were chosen among all the craftsmen in Israel to make the finest furnishings for the Tabernacle of Moses. Likewise, the sons of Asaph, poets and all the musicians associated with the Tabernacle of David revealed His Glory through song and spoken word. Thousands of craftsmen were called upon by Solomon to build the Temple where the Glory of the Lord came down in a cloud and overwhelmed all the people. Throughout history, artists have been called upon to reveal the story of the Gospel, the imagery of the Church, and the power of the promise of salvation.

As you embrace your own call as an artist in the Kingdom, you must realize that this involves more than simply reflecting what has happened or retelling the stories of history. There is great value in recounting the works of the Lord and in telling the stories of what God has done. As a reflector of the Glory of God however, you are called to show forth not only what has happened, but what is happening and what will happen! As one who is called to be "in-tune" with Holy Spirit and the voice of the Lord, you have been uniquely equipped to prophesy to the world the purposes of God in your generation.

Transmitting the Power of God

It is important to understand that prophecy is not just the communication of mere information. Prophetic utterance is literally the transmission of the power of God through revelation by the Holy Spirit. The word "prophecy" comes from the root word for "light" or "illumination." We must understand therefore, that Jesus is Who provides the illumination. Prophecy is a supernatural way of communication given to us by the Father to be a light in the earth and to be witness to the lost so they will come to know Jesus. Just as the two witnesses in Revelation chapter 11 were called, "Lampstands," so are we called to burn with the fire of God and bring illumination to a dark world!

Mark Nysewander, a spiritual giant in my life, said recently in a message at Riverstone Church,

> "We are a lampstand that holds the fire of God, the fire of His message and the fire of His presence. At the end of the age, when things are very dark and the anti-Christ is moving and judgments are falling – in that darkness, against that dark background will be the brilliance of the prophetic witness of the church! Because in that moment we will display the Light of His Message and the Light of His Presence."

Your creative expression has no choice but to be prophetic when it is infused with the power and unction of the Holy Spirit. Speaking the "now word" (rhema) of God into the earth at an appointed (kairos) time, confirmed by signs and wonders following, comes naturally as you take time to explore intimacy with the Father through worship, His Word, the Spirit and community with other believers. Only then will the creativity of your hands and heart reflect the fullness of God's Glory.

Hearing the Voice of the Lord

The first step in developing your prophetic voice as an artist is to get in touch with your ability to hear the voice of the Lord. In my own journey and in the lives of the countless artists I've worked with over the years, this happens as a result of focused, 'on-purpose' times with the Father in worship and soaking in His presence. As you sit at His feet, meditate on His Word and gaze at His beauty, the voice of the Lord becomes stronger and stronger.

Apostle Paul wrote in 1 Corinthians 12 about the gifts of God. What we refer to as the "revelatory" gifts include"

- **Personal or Corporate Prophecy.** A word of encouragement, exhortation or edification for an individual or group.
- **The Word of Knowledge.** Someone knowing a specific fact about another person which they would have no way of knowing in the natural. God reveals this in order to build faith in the receiver or to bring healing, deliverance, or encouragement that God is handling it!
- **The Word of Wisdom.** An individual is able to give the exact counsel needed in a situation, birthed from the heart of God.

While these three spiritual gifts are used by the Lord to speak to us, He also uses other important means. For example, seeing mental images or pictures, often called visions. Most are in the mind's eye, although some people see actual scenes before them.

(Think of Peter seeing the image of the clean and unclean animals in an open vision.) Another is seeing mental images of words written above a person, or actually hearing them in your spirit. (Think of Daniel interpreting the words Nebuchadnezzar had seen on the wall in his dream: *Mene, Mene, Tekel, Upharsin* [Daniel 5:25].)

God may speak through journaling in that one day you may realize that your personal notes have become God speaking a specific thing to you.   He may also communicate through general conversation as a person speaks directly to your heart with a message from God or some specific inspiration.

God also speaks through dreams.   Believers and non-believers alike may experience this as many examples are mentioned in the Bible. God also uses things which may seem odd like a billboard, a license plate or even the wording on the side of a truck.

The most important thing is that you <u>want</u> to hear from God and that you <u>expect</u> to hear from Him. It is OK to desire to prophesy and to grow in that gift. In fact, Paul wrote in 1 Corinthians 14:1, *"Pursue love, yet desire earnestly spiritual gifts, but especially that you may prophesy"* (NASB). Ask God to attune your senses and your spirit so that you will not miss what He says. Feast on His Word (Revelation 10) and give Holy Spirit the opportunity to illuminate His voice inside of you. Create an atmosphere where He can best be heard like devoted time alone to hear Him, praying in the Spirit, listening to good worship music, and prolonged periods of silence.

Beholding His Beauty

You may have heard the phrase, "you become what you behold." The more you behold God in worship and through His Word, gazing upon His beauty, learning to hear His voice and dreaming with Him, the more prophetic your creativity becomes. It turns into a natural outflow of your relationship with the Father.

One of the powerful models we see for this is in the life of King David when he expressed his heart to the Father in Psalm 27:4, *"One thing I ask of the LORD, this is what I seek: that I may dwell in the house of the LORD all the days of my life, to gaze upon the beauty of the LORD and to seek him in his temple."*

Jesus Culture does a great song by Matt Redman called "King of Wonders" that includes the line, "the more we see, the more we love you." God's presence is addictive. The more you see Him, the more you want to see Him. The more you hear His voice, the more you listen for it. God designed you so that your hunger for Him would never be satisfied. God is endless in beauty and glory, and the minute you think you have seen it all He's like, *"BAMM! Here's another facet of my beauty!"* As a creative person, you are wired to tell others about God's beauty and reveal His glory through your art. It is a divine setup!

For me, the best times to hear the Lord are when I am weaving a basket, looking for natural materials in the woods or alone at my keyboard writing a song. I use those times in my creative secret place to invite Holy Spirit to speak to me. I have discovered time and again that He is already there, waiting for me.

Your Unique Expression

People often want to lump us creative folk under the bland title of "artists." The reality is however, that every one of us has a very different way of expressing our heart and the Glory of God. This is the beauty of the Kingdom!

Early in our artistic pursuits, the enemy usually tries to sow doubt and unbelief in our hearts with junk like, "You will never be as good as them" or "Who do you think you are? Your art doesn't look like theirs; it will never sell" or "Your stuff is too weird for commercial appeal." So before we are even out of the gate, the enemy kills the very creative spark that God gave us as our own unique facet of His Glory.

If the enemy is doing that to you, recognize it as a lie from the pit of hell and begin to declare God's love, favor and creativity over your life. Learn to wield the sword of His Word; it is the only way to gain power over the enemy in this area. You must know what God says about you so that you can recognize the lies of the enemy and refute them.

What Do You Love?

I have always been fascinated with Appalachian folk art. For some reason, when I get up into the hills of North Carolina, Tennessee, North Georgia or Kentucky, I have an inner sense that "these are my people." It took me a while to understand that my love for basketry and folk art was God-given, not just some hobby I picked up along the way. Once I started to embrace and explore the possibilities for my unique expression in the Kingdom, the Father began to fling open doors of opportunity that intersected with my passions. Now I am involved in creative business ventures with people that I was connected with prophetically through my love of kudzu, my primary basket-weaving medium. The Father also strategically moved my family to the center of Appalachian folk art, Asheville, North Carolina. You see, God loves to blow my mind. I just have to trust Him enough to walk in my calling.

It is very important to embrace the uniqueness that God has placed on your life and art because it is the very thing He wants to use you in the most. Your art and uniqueness is what the enemy will attack the most in your life and seek to destroy. Part of developing your unique prophetic voice is to dive into the uniqueness of your expression under the guidance of the Holy

Spirit, asking Him to permeate every fiber of what you create. As you follow His lead, the Father will begin to arrange divine appointments and strategic alignments in the Kingdom that you never thought possible. This comes simply because you have trusted Him enough to listen to His voice, follow His lead and step out in your uniqueness.

Once you are connected to the Father through His Word, intimate worship, hearing His voice and pursuing your unique artistic expression, you are on the road to seeing God blow your mind. He waits for you to open up the door so He can flow through you. The Father's desire for you, His artist, is to co-labor with Him in the Kingdom, doing the things that He wants to do in the earth as you walk in daily relationship with Him inspired by His creativity and Spirit. His Word clearly says in Joshua 1:3, *"I will give you every place where you set your foot. . ."* (NIV). In the context of taking the Kingdom everywhere you walk, the Father chose artists to serve many different functions, some you may be comfortable with and others you may be more reticent to accept.

Journal and Discussion Questions

1. *How do you respond to being uniquely equipped to prophesy the purposes of God in your generation? Does this excite and inspire you or overwhelm you?*

2. *What are some of the ways God speaks to you? Dreams, visions, inspiration while creating?*

3. *What are the things that make you a unique prophetic voice in the Kingdom?*

4. *What are things the enemy attacks most in your life and creative expression?*

Chapter 8

Reveal the Testimony of Jesus

"When creativity is the normal expression of God's people there is something that happens to all who oppose Him. They become disheartened. The devil himself has no creative abilities whatsoever. All he can do is distort and deform what God has made. God is made known through His works. When His works flow through His children their identity is revealed, and there is an inescapable revelation of the nature of God in the land. He is irresistible to those who have eyes to see."[1]

The goal of revealing the person, message and nature of Jesus through the power of the Holy Spirit is central in your pursuit as an artist in the Kingdom. Revelation 19:10b states *"Worship God! For the testimony of Jesus is the spirit of prophecy"* (NKJV). The work of your hands, your own ego or the desire to build yourself up should never be the sole focus of your work. This only leads to emptiness! Rather, I would suggest you focus on being someone whom God uses to touch a generation and to reveal His Glory through the uniqueness of who He has created you to be. The

---

[1] Johnson, Bill. *Dreaming with God: Secrets to Redesigning Your World Through God's Creative Flow.* [S.l.]: Destiny Image, 2006. Print

Father longs to encourage you, build you up and to give you the desires of your heart, but it is never about you – it is about Him!

The Other Side of God's Glory

Over the years I have discovered that many people are very comfortable with the notion that an artist is someone who reveals the beauty and majesty of God through their artistic creation:

- a beautiful sculpture in bronze of a child
- a painting of a majestic mountain scene
- a work in hand-blown glass
- a song that speaks to the heart
- fabric and fiber arts

When it comes to God's glory however and the testimony of Jesus, some folk have difficulty with the artists' expression of God's truth.

What happens when the creative expression of God's artists turns into a message that is more prophetic in nature, calling out to humanity for change or severe adjustment in life or culture? What if the Father chooses to evoke a response that reveals the heart of a person? What happens when the Lord begins to use His co-creators in the Kingdom to express parts of His heart that can be difficult to hear?

As an artist in the Kingdom, it can be difficult to come to grips with God using your creative expression to speak to His people, yet this is what the Lord has required of His artists throughout the ages. The Father says of Bezalel (a craftsman from the tribe of Judah) *"I have filled him with the Spirit of God, giving him great wisdom, intelligence and skill in all kinds of crafts . . .he is a master at every craft!"* (Exodus 31:3,5b NLT). Bezalel was:

- filled with the Spirit of God and

- skilled in every craft

The musicians in the Tabernacle of David were described in the same way in that they played skillfully and prophesied before the Lord. God has always wanted artists and craftsmen to know His voice and to respond to Him through creative expression under the anointing of the Holy Spirit. As a craftsman, He calls you to respond as well!

The Blacksmith

As the Lord gave me more revelation on this subject, He led me to Isaiah 54:16-17 and the implications it holds for the calling of artists:

> "'Behold, I Myself have created the smith who blows the fire of coals And brings out a weapon for its work; And I have created the destroyer to ruin. No weapon that is formed against you will prosper; and every tongue that accuses you in judgment you will condemn. This is the heritage of the servants of the LORD, And their vindication is from Me,' declares the LORD." (NASB)

At nearly the same time the Lord showed me a passage of Scripture in Isaiah 44:10-12ff. Here He described the blacksmith again, along with a woodcarver, but this time they were making idols:

> "Who shapes a god and casts an idol, which can profit him nothing? He and his kind will be put to shame; craftsmen are nothing but men. Let them all come together and take their stand; they will be brought down to terror and infamy. The blacksmith takes a tool and works with it in the coals; he shapes an idol with hammers, he forges it with the might of his arm. He gets hungry and loses his strength; he drinks no water and grows faint." (NIV)

These two passages set craftsmen right in the middle of the redemptive purposes of God for Israel. The prophet used terminology that the people understood to describe God's goodness and His desire to redeem and prosper them. It is interesting how the Lord chose to have the prophet tell the story in the context of artists.

Isaiah went on to write about the uselessness of a craftsman who wastes his time and talent making idols that *"can profit him nothing"* (Isaiah 44:11 NIV). He painted a very vivid picture of how artists can engage in artistic and creative endeavors that were totally useless and even dangerous to them and the wider population. Isaiah described how this kind of work causes the craftsman to *"get hungry and lose his strength; he drinks no water and grows faint"* (vv 12 NIV). This is a vivid description of how artists can pursue art for art's sake and creation for creation's sake but are left totally empty, drained, hungry and faint at the end of their search.

What a clear picture of the lives of many artists today; struggling, searching, desiring yet left unfulfilled and wanting. Not only that, but their creation leads them, and others, away from the very Source of love they all seek.

Now let us look at Isaiah 54:16-17. Here the Father told Israel that it was He Who created the blacksmith and that it was He Who *"forms weapons against thee"* (vv 16 KJV). The Father showed Israel that whatever came their way, even attacks and difficult situations, were under the control and dominion of the Lord.

As artists, it is interesting to note that the Lord spoke of the blacksmith as an artist whom He created for His purposes on the earth, even purposes that may not have been easily understood by His people. The Lord created the blacksmith to create tools that brought pain and inflicted judgment. For many, this can be a little disconcerting and yet it is a perfect illustration of an aspect of the prophetic nature we fulfill as artists.

Christian Art or Prophetic Art?

A mistake made today by many Christians is to label only 'family-friendly' or 'G-rated' creative expression as Christian art or God-inspired. The truth is that the Father has chosen to use artists to express His heart throughout the generations in a variety of ways – some easy to understand and some difficult to understand. Become comfortable with the prophetic nature of your work. Then, when the Lord speaks, you are able to respond with no religious preconception of what that response should be.

With Signs & Wonders Following

Jesus said:

> *"And these signs will accompany those who believe: In my name they will drive out demons; they will speak in new tongues; they will pick up snakes with their hands; and when they drink deadly poison, it will not hurt them at all; they will place their hands on sick people, and they will get well."* - Mark 16:17

A natural outflow of being a Kingdom believer and artist is having signs and wonders follow you. The Bible is full of illustrations where the power and presence of God was everywhere. If Paul could send a handkerchief full of the power and presence of God to a person who was sick and they were healed, then so can you! Your work carries the very power and presence of God. Let faith arise and expect signs and wonders to follow your work, releasing the voice of God through your creative expression!

Glory Stories

I have a dear friend, Lynn Rinehart, who is a fiber artist and leader of The Worship Studio in metro Atlanta. The Lord gives Lynn dreams in the night of patterns and designs for quilts. She prays over every cut and stitch and has literally seen marriages healed when people sleep under the quilts she makes.

When I first began The Worship Studio in Atlanta an artist brought in one of her paintings. As she lay in bed gazing on this painting and crying out to the Lord for deliverance, she was healed from major depression. She then displayed it in the gallery hoping others would be healed as well.

Recently I heard a story about a woman with a stage four brain tumor who attended a healing room ministry at a church out west. While in the healing room she stood for a while looking at a painting entitled "Hope." As she looked at the painting, her tunnel vision cleared and the pressure in her head was relieved. Then a warm liquid began to run out of her ear. When she returned to her doctor he confirmed that she had no more cancer; the tumor was gone! Praise God!

At Riverstone, my former church in Kennesaw, Georgia, there is a prophetic art team led by artist June Littlepage. At their Nights of Healing Prayer, the artist team paints prophetically on 5x7 canvases as people are ministered to during the evening. Nearly every person who comes in for healing receives a personal prophetic word in art from an artist on the team. What a tangible reminder to that person of the love of God!

Here in Asheville I have a friend who is a world-renowned glass artist with work found in some of the finest hotels and homes around the world. The wonderful thing about his work is that much of what he produces comes directly out of visions of Glory that God gives him while he worships. The tangible presence of

God is not only inspiring, but literally resting in His pieces as they go out into the world.

All Matter Has Memory

According to my friend, author, musician and scientist David Van Koevering (www.elsewhen.com), all matter has memory and can retain what it sees and hears. That means your artistic expression, created in and with the presence of God, can literally carry His presence into the earth and effect change! This may be a 'quantum leap' for you, but there's much more to your creativity that just the sum of your creative tools and expression. There is a non-physical, spiritual reality that the Father has given us to live, move and create within. We are not just physical beings and the world we live in is not just a physical world! We are spirit, soul and body, equipped to engage creatively with the Father to reveal the testimony of Jesus on all levels.

Note: For many years, a good friend of mine David Van Koevering has done much research in the field of quantum physics and it's relation to the spiritual truths of the Bible. The revelation he's received from the Father is especially poignant for ones called to create. I've shared some of David's thoughts with you on the reality of the non-physical reality in which we live in the Appendix of this book called "There is a Non-Physical Reality". Please take some time to read and check out some of the other resources from ElseWhen.com.

Your creative calling is close to the heart of God. He is your creative Source. His is the voice in the night that awakens you with new inspiration and desire. Whether your creative expression is being used in the Kingdom to inspire, rebuke, encourage or warn, I pray that you, as an artist who loves Jesus, will grow ever closer to Him and become more aligned with His purposes for your generation. You may never become comfortable in your calling as a Kingdom artist, but as you grow in the prophetic nature of your calling you can rest assured that God speaks and expresses His heart through your art. That is indeed your calling in the Kingdom.

Journal and Discussion Questions

1. *Do you relate to the description in Isaiah 44 of artists who give themselves to artistic and creative endeavors that can be totally useless and even dangerous?*

2. *Have you ever felt the pressure to produce "Christian Art" when you sensed the Lord wanted to release a message that may have been more difficult for people to receive?*

3. *How do you walk the balance between artistic expression that is both edifying and challenging at the same time?*

4. *How does all matter having memory affect the impact of your artistic expression? Does this change your perspective on your work?*

Chapter 9
Prospering Artists, not Starving Artists

The first Gathering of Artisans we ever held at The Worship Studio in Georgia was a powerful time of worship, collaboration and ministry among artists young and old, master and emerging. We were all excited to see what God was doing among this new community of creative ones! As we worshipped that night, a painter I have known for years, Ginger Mosher (www.gemgallery.org) reminded us of a prophetic word the Lord had given her for that year. She said the Lord wanted us to know that *"this would be the year of the prospering artist, not the starving artist."* Our hearts leapt with excitement as we received this word from the Father, yet reality was very different for many artists in the room that night. While hope was still flickering inside the hearts of many, their lives were fraught with anxiety, frustration and fear over their financial provision and their ability to make a living with their art.

My own journey of provision as an artist was like that of many others; I struggled to understand how I would actually make money at what I do. As I have matured as an artist and believer, I have come to realize that the performance orientation I often identified with had a huge influence on how I lived my life, how I experienced the world around me and how I received from the Father.

For much of my life, I held several core beliefs about God's provision for my life that I have come to understand are simply untrue and unbiblical. They were the product of lies from the enemy regarding my upbringing, experience, religious tradition and family modeling, and were not the Father's desire for my life. Some of the lies were"

- If I want to get ahead in life I will have to work really hard
- I will never make a lot of money being an artist
- I need to get a real job to support my family and do my creative stuff on the side
- God's provision for my life was conditional on how much I "sowed"
- Creative people are not good with money or business
- If I want to be an artist get used to not having a lot of material possessions
- I should charge less for my work so people will buy more
- I will never be good enough to do this full-time
- I will never be as good as them
- In order to have enough money to serve God full-time, I will have to become successful enough in business to have all my financial needs met

The list of lies that artists believe can go on forever as it is one of the main tools the enemy uses against all believers in order to keep us in our place. The Father wants us to believe what He says about us and about our calling. Breaking ties with these ungodly beliefs takes repentance, focusing on what He says about us and learning to wield the sword of His Word against the lies of the enemy.

Fake It Until You Make It

Like most artists, a deep-seated performance mentality ruled my nature. From the time I was a little boy I learned that if I wanted people to like me I should perform. It started out innocently enough, singing at church or for family friends, but quickly seeped into other areas of my life. Friendships, relationships and my professional life were all affected. I believed that I had to look or act a certain way for people to accept me. This was not a good way to live because it became the way I interacted with God, so I began to perform for Him as well in order to be good enough for His love and provision. I believed that if I messed up God would not love me or provide for me.

Needless to say, that kind of ungodly belief system can spawn all kinds of lies in a person's life. Mix that with the horrendous relationship I had with my father, the death of my favorite piano teacher, the death of my grandfather and sexual abuse by a close relative of mine and I was setup for a major attack from the enemy...it was a perfect storm. The enemy began trying to eliminate me at a very young age and when he did not succeed he attempted to build an entire system of ungodly beliefs through my woundedness. These lies led me into a double life of seclusion, secrecy and addiction that followed me most of my teenage and adult life.

Tear Down the Old System

When I discovered the ungodly belief system I had created for my life, I was astounded by how it had affected my creativity, my family and my provision. It literally permeated every area of my life and held me as a frustrated, unfulfilled captive. As I pressed into the Father for understanding, He began to show me several key verses in His Word that shaped the way I viewed my relationship with Him and my beliefs about His provision for my life. One of the key passages of scripture is from Matthew 6:25-34 where Jesus talked about worrying and God's promise of provision.

This revelation came to me through a teaching by Gary Carpenter, a brother from Tulsa, Oklahoma (www.garycarpenter.org). He challenged what I had been taught about how the only way I would receive financially from the Father was through sowing and reaping. It works today just like it did then, but when Jesus taught about giving it was in the context of relationship. He basically said,

> Look, why are you guys so worried about provision for your life, what you are going to eat, drink, wear, where you will live, I have got this covered. You are children of God and because of that alone, He has promised to provide for you. Seek His kingdom first and everything else will fall into place.

Everybody Eats at Grandpa's Table

To illustrate the teaching, Gary told a wonderful story about growing up on his grandpa's farm. Every morning they would all gather at the breakfast table for pancakes, biscuits and gravy, country ham, bacon, sausage, eggs, fresh milk, coffee and orange juice. The room bustled with cousins, uncles and aunts as they prepared for the day's work, while his grandpa sat at the head of the table, eager to pass out the responsibilities for the day. Some men would drive the combines, others would stack the hay, the ladies would take care of the home, teenagers would tend to the smaller gardens, and the small children would sometimes grease the tractor wheels or do odd jobs around the farm. Once everyone had their job for the day they set off to the fields to work.

Some of the folks in the family worked really hard, but every now and then you would see someone dozing behind the barn. Nevertheless, everyone had a job that fit his or her abilities and experience. Some of the men who had grown up on the farm and had proven themselves faithful were now in charge of teams of men. Others who were just starting out had lesser responsibilities according to their skill level. Even the kids worked while grandpa watched over the whole operation. At the end of the day, Gary's grandma would step out onto the back porch of the old home place and ring a big dinner bell signaling to everyone on the farm that it was time to come in and eat…and boy did they eat! Dinner was fried chicken, mashed potatoes, three or four vegetables, biscuits, gravy and gallons of sweet tea to wash it down. To finish it all off, they brought out coconut cake, lemon meringue pie and other desserts and then ate until they were absolutely filled.

No matter what job you had been given, or even how well you had done it, you knew that at the end of the day the dinner bell would ring and you would once again eat until you could eat no more. Not only that, you also had a warm place to lay your head at night in a bed that was just for you. The point of the story is that everybody eats at grandpa's table.

The same thing is true in the Kingdom. No matter what your calling is, God has promised to provide for your every need. Jesus challenged us in Matthew 6 by asking us why we continue to worry about things that He has already covered! The Father's promise of provision is the same for us as Gary's grandpa's provision was for his family: *"I love you. You are mine, and I will provide for your every need so long as you are in my family and serving in my Kingdom."*

Journal and Discussion Questions

1. *What are some of the lies that you have believed about God's provision for your life and calling?*

2. *What results have your ungodly beliefs about money and God's provision produced in your life?*

3. *What is your reaction to God's promise of provision, protection and favor on your life?*

4. *Do you feel like an orphan, a servant or a son when it comes to God's promise of provision for you?*

Chapter 10

The Promise of Abundance

People often confuse what God has called them to do as being tied to their provision. Calling and provision however, are promised by the Father and are not in any way conditional for His children.

Unlike provision, increase and promotion in God's Kingdom is conditional and based upon how you manage what you have been given. In the story of the talents in Matthew 25:14 and following, a man gives talents to his servants *"each according to his own ability."* When the man returns, he examines the work of the servants and rewards the one who has invested his talents for him saying, *"Well done good and faithful servant. You have been faithful over a few things, I will make you ruler over many. Enter into the joy of your lord"* (vv 21).

Jesus illustrated this powerful truth that if you want increase and favor in His Kingdom you must use what He has given you. Dream, take calculated risks, step out to see God work mightily on your behalf! Anything less will be refused by the Father.

God Has Your Back

Are you getting this? Your provision is covered…it is a done deal! It is God's promise for you as His child and all you have to do is believe it by faith and receive it. Even more powerful is the fact that not only does God want to provide for you, He wants to prosper you based on the abilities and talents that He has given you. As you step out and dream with Him, you will see increase, promotion and favor like you have never known! Not only that, but you will enter into the joy of your Lord because you are working out of your passions and God-designed creativity, not out of fear of lack or your need for money.

Though it took a long time to get this revelation deep into my heart, once it happened, my reality shifted. I finally began to understand God's plan for provision, but not until I left full-time vocational ministry, started a boutique ad agency, chased hard after money and made some, and then lost almost everything. God had to bring me to the place where I trusted Him completely, but it was a long road of brokenness and healing. I can point back to a single point in time when all this clicked for me and I really began to believe that God had my back. That was when I realized He loved me and wanted me to succeed and to pursue the passions of my heart that He had deposited there.

I had been through a hellacious few years that included coming clean with a lifelong addiction to pornography, major betrayal by a business partner, losing my business, going through major personal and business financial turmoil, and almost losing everything I had materially. By 2008, God had sovereignly placed me at Cisco Systems in Atlanta. The upside was I had a stable job with great benefits. The downside was I had to be inside an office in a 5x5 cubicle every day, 8 hours a day, something this free spirit was not used to or inclined to enjoy. During this time, God started getting my attention, focusing on Him. It was coming up on 7 years since I had left full-time ministry and He was beginning to light the fire in me again.

Tanya and I had sensed a call to return to ministry, but were unsure about the direction. I applied at a number of different churches all over the country, and was contacted by quite a few who said they were interested in me or that I had made it to the top of their list, but by the end of December 2008, I still had not been offered a position. In January 2009, while still working at Cisco, I was laid off. This happened right after I won the "Game Changer for 2008" world-wide sales award! No notice, no severance, no nothing. "Thank you very much; you can leave right now" – along with 30% of the floor I worked on.

Popcorn Provision

Strangely enough, we were excited. We that knew God was up to something, but had no idea what specifically. We had just returned from a great church in New England and were anticipating an offer but at the last minute they said it would be another month before a decision was made.

Now I was confused. "God, have you brought me this far to leave me?" What was I going to do for money while I waited? The Father told me clearly "Don't look for a job, your provision will come like popcorn. I am turning up the heat and pouring in the oil." A little bit confused by the prospect of not providing for my family I asked the Lord what to do. He said "Lay on the floor, worship me and seek my face."

The very next day, people began to call me. . .

"Matt, we need a logo and website for our business, can you help?"

"Matt, I have a client that needs a brochure designed."

"Matt, I heard you are not working at Cisco anymore. A company in Kennesaw needs a contract Marketing Director with ministry, marketing and technology experience, are you interested?"

Literally like popcorn, the Lord began to bring creative work to me that I was passionate about and had tried to pursue in my own strength years before, but to no avail.

During this time the church in New England called and said they were ready to talk about moving forward. Now I was really confused. What was I to do? As I sought the Lord He came back with a question, "Is this church really your DNA?" I knew it was not. It was a great church, doing great things, but it was not my DNA. I had to make a hard choice, take a job that would pay almost six figures and provide free private school for my son, or stay in Atlanta and trust God to fulfill the desires of my heart. I chose to stay; what God did was amazing!

Ministry and Marketplace

One day soon after the decision to stay in Atlanta, I asked the Father about my calling: *"If I am going to stay here You have to show me what I am supposed to do!"* He told me very clearly that I was called fulltime to both ministry and marketplace. Not only did He start bringing work that paid well and was creatively engaging, I now had more flexibility in my schedule for ministry. People started calling me to lead worship at conferences and retreats... It was wild! Everything I had been longing for – creative expression, fulfillment in my work, passion, flexibility in my schedule for ministry – was coming at me like a wave!

Secrets of the Kingdom

During this season the Father started showing me through Bill Johnson's book, "Dreaming with God," that the secrets of the Kingdom were my inheritance (Luke 8:10). As I continued to seek the Lord about my calling, what I was designed for and what my role in the Kingdom was, He began to release the vision for The Worship Studio and to align me with people around the world who had the same vision. Men like Ray Hughes, David Van

Koevering and Dave Markee, who had been icons in my life and mentors from afar through their books and teachings, were now intersecting my life. We were being linked together in the Spirit to see the Kingdom come!

Within a matter of six months, my understanding of God's provision changed. I went from a frustrated, broken, unfulfilled creative person who was dying on the vine, to someone who was firing on all cylinders, pursuing my dreams and experiencing favor like never before. What was the difference? I chose what Jesus called the "better thing" – to pursue intimacy with Him, believe His Word, and to discard ungodly beliefs about what His provision was all about. I chose to believe that God loved me, wanted the best for me, really did want me to prosper and wanted to give me the desires of my heart. As I did those simple things, my reality began to change. Before, I had tried to make enough money to have the financial freedom to be able to serve God in ministry. The Lord showed me how backward my thinking was. His Word says, *"Seek first the Kingdom of God...and all these things will be added unto you"* (Matthew 6:33), not "seek your provision first and then you can serve in My Kingdom." God showed me that I must focus on my calling in the Kingdom and as I did provision would follow. Now I can imagine living no other way. This is a very different paradigm of life and ministry, a paradigm of freedom, faith and provision.

Grace to Shift

God did end up moving us out of Atlanta to the mountains of Western North Carolina. Now I serve as Worship Pastor among a people who share a common vision – to see the Kingdom established in our city. Asheville is also a center for a very large community of artists, musicians, Appalachian folk artists and the headquarters for the Southern Highland Craft Guild (one of the most influential fine craft guilds in the country which was started by people of faith with a vision for the economic empowerment of southern Appalachian artisans and economic transformation of the entire region).

Now, just about a year later, I am sitting atop a beautiful mountain in a fabulous home, telling you this story as the snow drifts slowly down the valley. I am at peace, fulfilled creatively in ministry and in business, and living in a city that is at the very center of God's plan for me. This year, we hosted our first Gathering of Artists weekend retreat where artists from 14 states around the country were in attendance and have seen many begin to lay hold of the vision for 'raising up an army of artists'. I continue to do freelance design work for clients around the country, and have just been granted membership in the Southern Highland Craft Guild as a fiber artist. I am also starting to write songs again! I could tell you story after story from this past year about how God has blown me away with what I call "embarrassing favor." It is His desire for you, too!

Today when I wake up I am no longer fearful or worried about my provision. God has taught me how to ride the wave of His presence and to use what is currently in my hand. Some days, I work at the church all day, while other days I will be in my studio weaving kudzu baskets. Whether I am training artists in The Worship Studio, leading worship, relaxing with my family or whatever else Father calls me to that day, I can rest assured that He has my back. When I do what He puts before me, I know that it will be the desire of my heart and that His promise to provide for me is sure.

Quite the Artist

This past summer I led worship at a youth conference. As I began sharing my life a lady laughed and said "Well, you are quite the artist, aren't you?" I have to admit that for the first time in my life

I said, "Yes. Yes, I am." I am not some disjointed, unable to focus, artistic weirdo who is being irresponsible. I am an artist in the Kingdom of Almighty God, fulfilling His unique calling on my life and flowing with Him as He leads me.

My friend, wherever you are on the journey as one of His creative ones, embrace your calling with full faith and belief that God's promise of provision, protection and favor for your life is sure. It is your inheritance as a child in His Kingdom. I encourage you to step out, dream again and believe God for all that He has for you! It is time for you to fulfill your calling as an artist in the Kingdom with no fear to hold you back!

NOTES: These verses in particular have been a source of strength for me and a set of signposts that have led the way to God's true plan for provision and favor for my life. I read them often and have made them a part of my daily quiet time with the Lord.

- *"As a man thinketh in his heart, so is he."* - Proverbs 23:7 (KJV)

- *"You will also decree a thing, and it will be established for you..."* - Job 22:28 (NASB)

The truth of God's Word works both ways in regards to creating the reality we experience. I was literally creating my own negative reality based on lies from the enemy.

- *"And you shall remember the Lord your God, for it is He who gives you power to get wealth."* - Deuteronomy 8:18

- *"Delight yourself in the Lord and he will give you the desires of your heart; Commit your way to the Lord, Trust also in Him, and He shall bring it to pass. . ."* - Psalm 37:4-7 (NASB)

- *"Seek first the Kingdom of God and His righteousness and all these things shall be added unto you."* - Matthew 6:33

- *". . . will he not much more clothe you, O you of little faith?"* - Matthew 6:30b

- *"To you it has been given to know the mysteries of the kingdom of God. . ."* - Luke 8:10

Journal and Discussion Questions

1. *What are the talents God has given you to serve Him in His Kingdom?*

2. *What unique expression of creativity has the Father entrusted to you?*

3. *Has God asked you to step out in faith in any area of your life that requires you to trust Him for your provision?*

4. *What do you believe God for in your life and in your creative endeavors? Come on! Dream a little!*

Chapter 11

Embrace Community

During the early spring of 2009, the Father began to give me a vision for The Worship Studio and how He wanted to raise up an army of artists to reveal His Glory on the earth. The vision was not so much about doing as it was about being: Artists being with artists in authentic, Spirit-led, creative community.

The reference point I had for the vision was the John C. Campbell Folk School, a wonderful creative community in Western North Carolina, where I am privileged to serve as a basketry instructor. In existence since 1925, the Folk School is located on a rural campus where, in true community, resident artists hold classes and seminars focused on training, encouraging and releasing artists in their creative medium of choice. My heart burned with fiery passion to help artists develop authentic and collaborative community, both in a place like the Folk School and around the world.

Our Heavenly Father yearns for communities of artists to arise in the spirit of Naioth Ramah (Samuel's School of the Prophets) and of the Tabernacle of David where life is centered on God's Glory. One day while scouring the Bible for additional revelation on the subject, the Lord revealed more about our history as artists in the community. Though it can be awkward for artists to pursue genuine community with one another, we have a strong history both in the church and throughout history, of living, working and collaborating together in guilds and creative organizations. A passage in Nehemiah even refers to a physical place called "The Valley of the Craftsmen" where all the artists and craftsmen lived during the rebuilding of the Temple.

Band of Brothers

Wikipedia says this about the early guilds:

> "In pre-industrial cities, craftsmen tended to form associations based on their trades, confraternities of textile workers, masons, carpenters, carvers, glass workers, each of whom controlled secrets of traditionally imparted technology, the 'arts' or 'mysteries' of their crafts. Usually the founders were free independent master craftsmen."[2]

Guilds or other formal gatherings of artists can be dated to as early as AD 300-600 in Roman, Greek, Persian, Indian and Early European communities. Although most of these guilds were formed for business advancement, protecting trade secrets and developing skills, artists have always gathered to share, support and encourage one another, even when it was not encouraged or understood by the Church. "The early egalitarian communities called 'guilds' (for the gold deposited in their common funds) were denounced by Catholic clergy for their 'conjurations'—the binding oaths sworn among artists to support one another in

---

[2] "Guild." *Wikipedia, The Free Encyclopedia.* Wikimedia Foundation, Inc. 14 February 2011. 16 February 2011

adversity and back one another in feuds or in business ventures."
3

We artists often misunderstand that gathering together for mutual support and collaboration is essential to our ability to move into God's perfect plan. As Kingdom people, we are knit together as the Body of Christ to work together. No individual has all the inspiration, ability, creativity or understanding to walk in the fullness of what God has for our generation, which is why Paul taught the Corinthian church about the Body of Christ and the concept of being interconnected. Following is a long portion of Scripture, but take a moment to really get this in your spirit as it is the basis of God's design for healthy community:

> *"God's various gifts are handed out everywhere; but they all originate in God's Spirit. God's various ministries are carried out everywhere; but they all originate in God's Spirit. God's various expressions of power are in action everywhere; but God himself is behind it all. Each person is given something to do that shows who God is: Everyone gets in on it, everyone benefits. All kinds of things are handed out by the Spirit, and to all kinds of people! The variety is wonderful:*
> *"wise counsel*
> *clear understanding*
> *simple trust*
> *healing the sick*
> *miraculous acts*
> *proclamation*
> *distinguishing between spirits*
> *tongues*

---

[3] "Guild." *Wikipedia, The Free Encyclopedia*. Wikimedia Foundation, Inc. 14 February 2011. 16 February 2011

interpretation of tongues.

"All these gifts have a common origin, but are handed out one by one by the one Spirit of God. He decides who gets what, and when.

"You can easily enough see how this kind of thing works by looking no further than your own body. Your body has many parts—limbs, organs, cells—but no matter how many parts you can name, you're still one body. It's exactly the same with Christ. By means of his one Spirit, we all said good-bye to our partial and piecemeal lives. We each used to independently call our own shots, but then we entered into a large and integrated life in which he has the final say in everything. (This is what we proclaimed in word and action when we were baptized.) Each of us is now a part of his resurrection body, refreshed and sustained at one fountain—his Spirit—where we all come to drink. The old labels we once used to identify ourselves—labels like Jew or Greek, slave or free—are no longer useful. We need something larger, more comprehensive.

"I want you to think about how all this makes you more significant, not less. A body isn't just a single part blown up into something huge. It's all the different-but-similar parts arranged and functioning together. If Foot said, 'I'm not elegant like Hand, embellished with rings; I guess I don't belong to this body,' would that make it so? If Ear said, 'I'm not beautiful like Eye, limpid and expressive; I don't deserve a place on the head,' would you want to remove it from the body? If the body was all eye, how could it hear? If all ear, how could it smell? As it is, we see that God has carefully placed each part of the body right where he wanted it.

"But I also want you to think about how this keeps your significance from getting blown up into self-importance. For no matter how significant you are, it is only because of what you are a part of. An enormous eye or a gigantic hand wouldn't be a body, but a monster. What we have is one body with many parts, each its proper size and in its proper place. No part is important on its own. Can you imagine Eye telling Hand, 'Get lost; I don't need you'? Or, Head telling Foot, 'You're fired; your job has been phased out'? As a matter of fact, in practice it works the other way—the 'lower' the part, the more basic, and therefore necessary. You can live without an eye, for instance, but not without a stomach.

"When it's a part of your own body you are concerned with, it makes no difference whether the part is visible or clothed, higher or lower. You give it dignity and honor just as it is, without comparisons. If anything, you have more concern for the lower parts than the higher. If you had to choose, wouldn't you prefer good digestion to full-bodied hair?

"The way God designed our bodies is a model for understanding our lives together as a church: every part dependent on every other part, the parts we mention and the parts we don't, the parts we see and the parts we don't. If one part hurts, every other part is involved in the hurt, and in the healing. If one part flourishes, every other part enters into the exuberance.

"You are Christ's body—that's who you are! You must never forget this. Only as you accept your part of that body does your "part" mean anything.

"You're familiar with some of the parts that God has formed in his church, which is his 'body'." - 1 Corinthians 12:4-28 (MSG)

The Father's design is for artists to be part of a well-oiled machine, an army marching together to impact culture on a global scale through His Glory. God has called us to take back the mountain of arts and entertainment! To do this, each of us must take the call to community seriously. This is about our survival, not our comfort.

Understanding your role in the body of Christ and the safety it offers is vital to your success. You were never meant to walk this road of life and creativity alone! Community is at the core of God's end-time purposes for you as one of His creative ones! The Father is calling you even now to join with the Holy Spirit in this generation to see Glory released in and through you!

Culture War

We are in a spiritual battle for the hearts of artists and the soul of our culture. The Bible is clear; *"...we are not fighting against people made of flesh and blood, but against the evil rulers and authorities of the unseen world, against those mighty powers of darkness who rule this world, and against wicked spirits in the heavenly realms"* (Ephesians 6:12 NLT). It is crucial, therefore, that we understand how to wisely engage in battle in this time.

When you research the study of War, you find that many military strategists have attempted to encapsulate a successful strategy in a set of principles. Sun Tzu defined thirteen principles in "The Art of War" while Napoleon listed 115 maxims. American Civil War General, Nathan Bedford Forrest, had only one: *"to git thar furst with the most men."* The concepts listed as essential in the United States Army Field Manual of Military Operations (FM-3-0, Sections 4-32 to 4-39) are:

1. **Objective** (Direct every military operation toward a clearly defined, decisive, attainable objective)
2. **Offensive** (Seize, retain, and exploit the initiative)
3. **Mass** (Concentrate combat power at the decisive place and time)
4. **Economy of Force** (Allocate minimum essential combat power to secondary efforts)
5. **Maneuver** (Place the enemy in a disadvantageous position through the flexible application of combat power)
6. **Unity of Command** (For every objective, ensure unity of effort under one responsible commander)
7. **Security** (Never permit the enemy to acquire an unexpected advantage)
8. **Surprise** (Strike the enemy at a time, at a place, or in a manner for which he is unprepared)
9. **Simplicity** (Prepare clear, uncomplicated plans and clear, concise orders to ensure thorough understanding)[4]

To better understand how God wants to form an army of artists, focus your attention on strategies three, four and five – Mass, Economy of Force and Maneuver.

Mass is the concept of concentrating combat power at the decisive place and time, and moving together as one unit with one vision and one purpose.

Economy of Force is to keep the main thing the main thing! Do not waste effort or resources on secondary items. Focus on the goal and work toward it effectively and in unity.

Maneuver means to be flexible in attack. We must never become so entrenched in the methodology that we forget our

---

[4] *U.S. Army Field Manual: Military Operations.* Arlington, VA: Association of the United States Army, 2007. Print

ultimate purpose. Our purpose as artists is to see God move in and through us to reveal His glory and presence on the earth, and to see the hearts of people redeemed and restored. We must never take our eyes off that goal and we must never forget that it is impossible to accomplish this alone!

By now, I trust you have apprehended the idea of embracing community, not only for your own growth, but for the greater purpose as the culture is impacted. More than that however, I want you to understand the heritage that is yours in creative community.

Bezalel and Oholiab in the Tabernacle of Moses

The first instance in the Bible where we see artists at work under the inspiration of the Holy Spirit is in Exodus 31:

Then the LORD said to Moses, "See, I have chosen Bezalel son of Uri, the son of Hur, of the tribe of Judah, and I have filled him with the Spirit of God, with skill, ability and knowledge in all kinds of crafts- to make artistic designs for work in gold, silver and bronze, to cut and set stones, to work in wood, and to engage in all kinds of craftsmanship. Moreover, I have appointed Oholiab son of Ahisamach, of the tribe of Dan, to help him. Also I have given skill to all the craftsmen to make everything I have commanded you: the Tent of Meeting, the ark of the Testimony with the atonement cover on it, and all the other furnishings of the tent- the table and its articles, the pure gold lampstand and all its accessories, the altar of incense, the altar of burnt offering and all its utensils, the basin with its stand- and also the woven garments, both the sacred garments for Aaron the priest and the garments for his sons when they serve as priests, and the anointing oil and fragrant incense for the Holy Place. They are to make them just as I commanded you." (vv 1-11 NIV)

At this point in history, we see craftsmen from many tribes coming together to build the Tabernacle furnishings under the inspiration of the Holy Spirit. God chose Bezalel, the best of the best from the crowd and joined him with an apprentice to help him. This is a great picture because authentic community in the Kingdom is about fathering others and not competition and fear. It appears that Bezalel, the most talented, anointed artist around, was willing to lay down his own pride, ego and even viable commercial opportunities to serve the Lord with his talent, all the while raising up others to do the same.

Sons of Asaph in the Tabernacle of David

Another beautiful description of artists in community was when David set apart the musicians for service in the Tabernacle:

"David, together with the commanders of the army, set apart some of the sons of Asaph, Heman and Jeduthun for the ministry of prophesying, accompanied by harps, lyres and cymbals. Here is the list of the men who performed this service:

From the sons of Asaph:

Zaccur, Joseph, Nethaniah and Asarelah. The sons of Asaph were under the supervision of Asaph, who prophesied under the king's supervision.

As for Jeduthun, from his sons:

Gedaliah, Zeri, Jeshaiah, Shimei, Hashabiah and Mattithiah, six in all, under the supervision of their father Jeduthun, who prophesied, using the harp in thanking and praising the LORD. As for Heman, from his sons:

Bukkiah, Mattaniah, Uzziel, Shubael and Jerimoth; Hananiah, Hanani, Eliathah, Giddalti and Romamti-Ezer; Joshbekashah, Mallothi, Hothir and Mahazioth. All these were sons of Heman the king's seer." - 1 Chronicles 25:1-5 (NIV)

The Sons of Asaph existed as a brotherhood for years after their service in the Tabernacle ended because they were knit together in community as fathers pursuing their skill as led by the Spirit of God. What a great picture of how community yields longevity. Pursue community to leave a legacy.

Within the Tabernacle community you also see Godly authority established and honored. David, as the head, appointed the masters, Asaph, Jeduthan and Heman, and they in turn equipped the worshippers in song, prophetic utterance and instruments. It is interesting to note that as Godly order is honored and established more freedom and anointing is released!

As we embrace community, we must also pursue several core principles in the Kingdom that make it function, including:

Honor One Another

We must honor the gifts and anointing in each other. If we have problems with each other we must go to one another in the spirit of Matthew 18 and address issues in private and in love. We must encourage each other and build each other up in the Lord. As we honor each other and the Lord in authentic community, He will pour out increased favor and blessing on our life together. David realized this as He flowed with other creative ones in the Tabernacle. Psalm 133:

"A song of ascents. Of David.

How good and pleasant it is when brothers live together in unity! It is like precious oil poured on the head, running down on the beard, running down on Aaron's beard, down upon the collar of his robes.

It is as if the dew of Hermon were falling on Mount Zion. For there the Lord bestows his blessing, even life forevermore."

How encouraging! As we honor each other and pursue unity among us, the Father promises His anointing, blessing and life evermore!

Raise Up the Next Generation

When the Lord told me to "raise up an army of artists to reveal His Glory on the earth," He made it very clear that I was to equip the warriors and the weaklings, the master artists and the emerging artists, together (Joel 3:9-12). This is called spiritual fathering like we see with Paul and Timothy, Jesus and the disciples, Bezalel and Oholiab, Asaph and the Sons of Asaph, Samuel and the school of the prophets at Naioth Ramah. It is God's design. It is also God's mandate in Malachi 4:6 that we turn our hearts toward the spiritual children and emerging artists in our midst in order to fully realize the blessing of God in our midst. We must pour ourselves out in service to the next generation to see them fulfill their purposes in their generation.   Spiritual fathering and mothering springs forth out of a love for God, for the Kingdom and for those to whom God has called us. There is no place for fear and no place for holding back.

Clear Vision and Purpose

As we pursue community, we must know clearly what we are about and where we are going. Dave Markee, in his foundational book, "The Lost Glory," said:

"In the days ahead, God will call men and women
to form whole communities of artists and

musicians to pioneer a new Levitical order...They will pursue not only artistic excellence and pioneer new things in creativity, but also spur one another on to reach new heights in creative thought and discipline – the kind of 'coloring outside the lines' so loved by God. They will love God with their whole hearts and pursue His presence with all their might, being fully committed to wholeness and the true freedom that comes from the Spirit of God . . . As God raises up new communities of artists, these groups will be like wells of blessing in the earth. The ones who will last will be wise enough to center themselves around ministries that can properly care for them and support them in their quest."

What vision!! To encourage, love, spur on, collaborate, support, and heal! You and I are called to be wells of blessing on the earth! Unless we know and articulate the vision of why we gather in community, it just becomes another meeting to attend. This Kingdom journey is not just some meeting we go to, it is the way we choose to live our lives. It is the adventure of flowing with the Spirit of God!

Walk in Wholeness

Lastly, real community embraces and values the wholeness of each person. As each of us pursues authentic community we must embrace our call to minister wholeness, love and reconciliation to one another. We are the hands and feet of Jesus on the earth. When one is hurting we are those called to minister healing and hope.

As we walk-out our own journey from brokenness to wholeness, it is imperative to remember that wholeness and healing is tied to community. It is not an option. In James

5:16, the writer exhorts the people saying, *"Therefore confess your sins to each other and pray for each other so that you may be healed…"*

I burn with a vision to see communities of artists springing up all over the world. Like wells of blessing and springs of living water pouring forth out of the dry and broken places, these communities will embody God's creativity.

As we give ourselves to the Father through authentic community and to the vision He is calling us to, we will see the Glory of God invade culture, shake cities and change nations!

Journal and Discussion Questions

1. *What is your initial response to the call to community? Do you resist or embrace the call?*

2. *Where do you see yourself, your art, in the big picture of The Body of Christ? What part has God called you to play?*

3. *As one called to war in the heavenlies through inspired creative expression, which of the principles of war mentioned earlier do you most identify with? Which is the most challenging for you to embrace?*

4. *How has God called you to raise up the next generation?*

5. *What are some real ways you pursue authentic community among other artists in your circle of influence.*

Chapter 12

Glory to Glory: The Artist and Spiritual Discipline

The thought of an artist discussing the topic of spiritual discipline is a bit humorous to me. Artists are typically not inclined to pour energy into the rigorous pursuit of an ordered life. Most artists I know are like me in that they enjoy the free-spirited life that comes with the title. The reticence I felt to pursue more discipline was because of my own preconceived notions about how it would manifest. I liked who I was and quite frankly did not want to do anything to cramp my style, no matter how spiritual.

My artistic pursuits were never something I had to work hard at to excel. I rarely practiced anything and just flew by the seat of my pants. As a child I took piano for about seven years, but as a professional musician and worship pastor, I played by ear using chord charts. And voice lessons? Please! I had enough of that mess when I was growing up. I was in every chorus, quartet and small ensemble available learning to sing with proper technique. I was finally able to flow in the Spirit as I led worship without having to worry about all that technical mumbo jumbo.

The same was true in nearly every other area of my life as well, from my physical body to my time with the Lord, my relationship with my wife to my own study in college and graduate school. I lived life on autopilot and loved it. I was cruising along just fine thank you very much. In fact, I was the fair-haired child in every circle I was in. People loved me and commented on how talented, mature and anointed I was. Why should I change anything? As a worship pastor in my mid-twenties I remember thinking, *"Wow, I have this thing down. Some people just have it, I guess."*

Go Deeper

God's desire for us leads us into the future in light of our calling. He is not concerned with just our current circumstances and shortcomings, but with our entire existence.

Someone once told me to walk humbly because "Your talent can take you where your character can't keep you." How true! As to be expected God had a deeper work to do in my life. Although I was anointed and talented with gifts He had given me, my natural talents were taking me to places my character could not keep me. I was about to enter the threshing floor of preparation for what God had for me.

At the top of my game (in a great church, recording a CD, writing music, traveling to Africa on mission trips) I was hit with the greatest fear of my life – I could no longer sing. In fact, it was worse than that, not only was I unable to sing, but when I did sing it sounded bad. I had blown out my voice, developed two opposing polyps on my vocal folds and was facing major vocal surgery. One of the best surgeons in the country said the polyps were some of the largest he had ever seen. Even in my brokenness I was an overachiever!

To help heal the damage done to my vocal cords, I began a training regimen that continues to this day and helps me keep my voice healthy and strong. I focus on using proper support, breath control, and make healthier dietary choices designed to position myself for success. I also found a vocal coaching team that taught me how to sing rock music and really lay it out there without blowing out my voice.

Now, almost ten years later, I sound better, have more vocal stamina and have lost thirty pounds of excess weight. The Lord showed me through that difficult experience that I had to cultivate discipline in my life if I wanted to be in this for the long haul as a worship leader and a father to artists.

Skill Births Freedom

For some artists things may come naturally like it did for me. I would venture to say however, that the masters in their craft, the best of the best, did not simply get there overnight or by simply "flowing in the Spirit." They became masters because of focus, discipline and a willingness to exert the necessary effort to move to the next level.

Look, for example, at Tiger Woods. With all the wounds that have manifested in his life he is still the best golfer in the world. Not only that, but daily he focuses on the basics; his swing, putting, chipping and driving the ball. Likewise, the best musicians I know are those who can play any song in any key at any time because they know every scale – major, minor and chromatic – in every key. They are prepared, practiced and skilled at their craft.

The idea that God just wants you to do your best without investing a lot of work and skill is just a load of bunk. God is a God of excellence, majesty and beauty! The pursuit of excellence in your craft not only makes you better, it glorifies Him and reveals part of His nature to those who view your work and watch the story of your life.

The Father encourages us throughout His Word to give ourselves over to excellence, to press in, to go for it! Here are a couple of verses that really exhort us to give 110% to our life in the Kingdom:

> *"Do you not know that in a race all the runners run, but only one gets the prize? Run in such a way as to get the prize. Everyone who competes in the games goes into strict training. They do it to get a crown that will not last; but we do it to get a crown that will last forever."* - 1 Corinthians 9:24-25 (NIV)

> *"Exercise daily in God—no spiritual flabbiness, please! Workouts in the gymnasium are useful, but a disciplined life in God is far more so, making you fit both today and forever. You can count on this. Take it to heart. This is why we've thrown ourselves into this venture so totally."* - 1 Timothy 4:7-8 (MSG)

Spiritual Disciplines

Over the two thousand years of church history, Christians from every sect, movement and denomination have adopted what most of us have come to know as the "spiritual disciplines." Manuel Luz, in his book "Imagine That", said:

> "Spiritual Disciplines were conceived by early Christ followers as a means of training themselves, over the course of their lifetimes, toward increasing Christ-likeness."

The classic spiritual disciplines as outlined by Richard Foster in his work, *"Celebration of Discipline: The Path to Spiritual Growth"* (which you should read if you have not) are divided in the following manner:

- **The Inward Disciplines**
  - Meditation
  - Prayer

- o Fasting
- o Study
- **The Outward Disciplines**
  - o Simplicity
  - o Solitude
  - o Submission
  - o Service
- **The Corporate Disciplines**
  - o Confession
  - o Worship
  - o Guidance
  - o Celebration

As you meditate on the life of Jesus, you will discover a beautiful balance as He pursued these disciplines to align Himself with the purposes of His Father. Like Jesus,

"Christians over the years have learned that certain disciplines and practices help them keep the spiritual channels open and help keep the heart turned toward God. These disciplines can't save you; they can't even make you a holy person. But they can heighten your desire, awareness, and love of God by stripping down the barriers that you put up within yourself and some that others put up for you. What makes something a spiritual discipline is that it takes a specific part of your way of life and turns it toward God. A spiritual discipline is, when practiced faithfully and regularly, a habit or regular pattern in your life that repeatedly brings you back to God and opens you up to what God is saying to you".[5]

---

[5] Longman, Robert Jr. "Spiritual Disciplines and Practices." *Simplicity, Quiet, Time, and Devotion.* 18 February 2010. 16 February 2011.

It is also important to realize that practicing spiritual disciplines in your life does not merit favor, make you more spiritual, or get you brownie points in heaven. You are already totally loved and completely accepted by the Father through the work of Christ! You are His child and He loves you. The disciplines are simply external behaviors or habits to help bring about internal change and align you with God's purpose for your life.

Life-Giving Habits

From my own journey, I have found several other disciplines that are life-producing as I pursue my call as an artist in the Kingdom. These disciplines or habits are the same "Five Smooth Stones" I encouraged you to adopt in the Introduction at the beginning of our journey. Nevertheless, they warrant repeating here for your encouragement:

- Journaling
- Soaking in Worship & Prayer
- Community
- Creative Space
- Reading God's Word

Before you jump head-long into keeping a bunch of rules or adding several new things to your life, ask the Lord which of the disciplines are for you at this season. The last thing you want is to become burdened or attempt to make your life mirror some monastic model of holiness. Nevertheless, it is important for you to find a pattern of spiritual growth and a set of habits that make sense for you. No matter who you are, or where you have been, you need the practice of life-giving, Spirit-led disciplines in your life.

You are Bent

Man was created to be in fellowship and communion with God in a vertical relationship in order to see God's Kingdom established on the earth in horizontal relationship with those around him. The fall of man put everyone into a position of "bent-ness" toward the created, rather than the Creator. God's pursuit of you and me is a relentless wooing and romancing affair that calls us back to a place of intimate communion with Him.

> "Spiritually and psychologically, man is bent. The unfallen position was a vertical one, one of standing erect, face turned upward to God in a listening-speaking relationship. It was a position of receiving continually one's true identity from God. But fallen man is bent toward the creature and trapped in the continual attempt to find his identity in the created one rather than in the Uncreated."[6]

Pursuit of a centered, balanced life through spiritual discipline is in cooperation with God's pursuit of your heart.

You are Passionate

Each of us is prone to vulnerability because of our passionate nature as artists. *"We as artists seem to feel more deeply than most. Our summers seem sunnier, our winters seem colder, our highs higher, our lows lower. And our susceptibility to pleasure and fame and temptation seems higher. That is why we have such a need for spiritual discipline and grounding."* [7] It is in the practice of spiritual discipline in the quiet places of our life that we are able to build ourselves up in our most holy faith and strengthen our hearts to withstand the swirl of attack and temptation often

---

[6] Payne, Leanne. *The Healing Presence.* Eastbourne: Kingsway, 1990. Print

[7] Luz, Manuel. *Imagine That.* Moody, 2009. Print

thrown at us by the enemy. If time is not spent in the secret place developing intimacy with the Lord we will fall into temptation. It is not a matter of if, but a matter of when.

Artists are passionate by design with creative spirits that must be directed toward something to find an outlet. *"If [we] do not practice the presence of God, we will practice the presence of another."[8]* The fact that you are reading this book says you want God's very best for your life! To practice another presence is idolatry and definitely not God's best.

Called to Steward the Gift

The Father has given you beautiful, extravagant gifts, each according to your ability to steward them. Jesus said,

> *"Again, it will be like a man going on a journey, who called his servants and entrusted his property to them. To one he gave five talents of money, to another two talents, and to another one talent, each according to his ability."* - Matthew 25:14-15 (NIV)

Cultivating a deeper relationship and intimacy with God through the practice of spiritual disciplines expands your ability to steward your gifts and talents. This greater ability invites God to expand your area of influence and then trust you with more. Jesus went on with the story saying, *"His master replied, 'Well done, good and faithful servant! You have been faithful with a few things; I will put you in charge of many things"* (vv 21).

---

[8] Payne, Leanne. *The Healing Presence.* Eastbourne: Kingsway, 1990. Print

Called to Communicate His Glory

The very essence of your purpose is to reveal and release the Glory of God on the earth through your unique creative expression. The prophet Isaiah declared:

> *"Sing to God a brand-new song,*
> *sing his praises all over the world!*
> *Let the sea and its fish give a round of applause,*
> *with all the far-flung islands joining in.*
> *Let the desert and its camps raise a tune,*
> *calling the Kedar nomads to join in.*
> *Let the villagers in Sela round up a choir*
> *and perform from the tops of the mountains.*
> *Make God's glory resound."* - Isaiah 42:10-12a (MSG)

Rory Noland, in *"Heart of the Artist"* encourages us in this calling through the pursuit of the disciplines:

"When we immerse ourselves in God's Word, we grow spiritually and He equips us to do what He's called us to do. We need to look at the discipline of the quiet time as part of our training to minister as God's mouthpiece. We need to be students of God's Word the way we are students of our craft."[9]

Art as a Spiritual Discipline

Numerous artists over the years have told me that their time in the studio either alone in the creative flow or in collaboration with fellow artists, is the most spiritually connected time they have all week. This time invested with God is what makes it possible to tap into His nature and purpose for your life. Synergy is created that propels you further than you could ever go by yourself.

---

[9] Noland, Rory. *The Heart of the Artist: A Character-building Guide for You & Your Ministry Team.* Grand Rapids, MI: Zondervan Pub. House, 1999. Print

"The creation and expression of art can be a spiritual discipline for the artist. For if spiritual disciplines are indeed external behaviors that aid in internal transformation in an individual, then the activities of art - which are transcendent in nature - can be, and should be, a spiritual discipline for the artist who follows Christ. The intention of the artist should be to express his faith through his art; where God meets him, molds him, uses him and draws the artist to Himself. We must yield our art to God, and allow Him to change us through it, in intentional and disciplined ways."[10]

Ask the Lord to help you develop spiritual disciplines and life-giving habits in your life and you will experience an explosion of creativity and Spirit-led flow. Your artistic expression will go to the next level, and then higher than you ever dreamed as you intentionally connect with the One who created you! God is your ultimate inspiration, guide and goal.

---

[10] Luz, Manuel. *Imagine That.* Moody, 2009. Print

Journal and Discussion Questions

1. *Do you naturally embrace spiritual disciplines or lean more toward life on auto-pilot?*

2. *How do you respond to the assertion that skill births freedom?*

3. *What spiritual disciplines do you currently employ in your daily routine?*
    Which ones do you sense a connection with?

4. *Do you view your creative expression as a spiritual discipline? Why or why not?*

5. *Does your creative expression help center you in the Lord so you can hear His voice or does it cause spiritual distraction?*

Chapter 13

Worshipping the Work of Our Very Own Hands

As an artist with a desire for beauty and an eye for detail, a big part of the joy I experience in my creative process is seeing the end result. I can remember the first time I went to a pottery class as a young teenager, longing for the day when I would be allowed to throw on an actual pottery wheel. The anticipation was intense as I imagined the glorious vessels that would come from my immensely talented thirteen year old hands. (Yes, that was a joke!) It is funny to think about now, but that was the beginning of a life-long passion for crafts and making beautiful, functional objects with my hands.

After several years, I became pretty good and transitioned into other creative mediums including stone carving, wood carving, leather work and basketry, all with a natural twist. Something inside of me longed for this stuff. On the outside everyone knew me as a musician, but making things with my hands was where I spent most of my free time. As I graduated from high school and entered college, music was the thing I did, and even got paid for it, but hand-made crafts had captured my attention and drew me in ever deeper to its creative web.

The Kudzu Patch

I was in college the first time I was paid for one of my baskets. Behind my apartment building at the University of Georgia I discovered a kudzu patch. I had found a discarded English Willow Basketry book at the bookstore where I worked and used it to learn how to weave. Slowly but surely I turned these gnarly vines into something beautiful, functional and desirable. At first it was some of the ladies at work who wanted my baskets and then it spread to my friends. People actually wanted to buy my baskets! I remember the intense feeling of pride as I recognized that I had a gift that very few other people had.

That sense of pride and happiness flowed through to my musical endeavors as well. I have always been a singer, worship leader, keyboardist and songwriter. At least it seems like always as I have been playing, singing and performing since I was five years old. For me, it was as much a part of my DNA as my hair or eye color. Creative expression was a part of who I was at my very core. I cannot count the times that I was asked to sing, play the piano or perform in some way at family events, church gatherings or school functions. From an early age my identity as a performer was set.

You may feel the same way. You may feel that your creative expression is much more than just something you do, that it is at the core of who you are, how you live, why your heart beats. This is exactly how God created you. He created you to live your life seeking to reflect His Glory through your creative gifting.

Yet for me, and I suspect for most artists, a great challenge arises – the challenge to worship the Creator and not the created work. Even more challenging for me was the temptation to worship the identity I had as an artist and musician, rather than walking in humility before the Lord and men.

Tempted to Worship

For as long as there have been artists, musicians and creative ones, the temptation to worship self and the work of their hands has been present. It is very easy to believe that who we are and what we do, the songs we sing or the things we create are all done by us, for us and through us. At our core, each of us has a desire to believe that the universe really does revolve around us. That dangerous belief births pride and arrogance which ultimately results in more brokenness in our lives.

Lucifer was created as "the seal of perfection" (Ezekiel 28:12). Many scholars believe that the Bible refers to Lucifer as the angel who covered the throne of God with worship and was created with instruments inside his very being.

> "The workmanship of thy tabrets and of thy pipes was **prepared in thee** in the day that thou wast created. Thou art the anointed cherub that covereth; and I have set thee so: thou wast upon the holy mountain of God; thou hast walked up and down in the midst of the stones of fire." - vv 13b-14 (KJV; emphasis added)

The prophet Isaiah wrote about how Lucifer fell from heaven:

> "How you have fallen from heaven, O morning star, son of the dawn! You have been cast down to the earth, you who once laid low the nations! You said in your heart, 'I will ascend to heaven; I will raise my throne above the stars of God; I will sit enthroned on the mount of assembly, on the utmost heights of the sacred mountain. I will ascend above the tops of the clouds; I will make myself like the Most High.' But you are brought down to the grave, to the depths of the pit." - Isaiah 14:12-15 (NIV)

Lucifer's sin was not that he was beautiful, talented and creatively brilliant; those were things that the Father gifted Him with so that he could fill the heavens with worship before the Throne. The sin was Lucifer's desire to see himself and that which he created raised to equality with God. Bottom line; Lucifer believed that seeking his way, his desire and his pleasure separate from the Father would bring him fulfillment and happiness. However, this is what brought him, and many others, down into death and destruction. Sadly, that same lie entangles us today.

Have you listened to the lies of the enemy that would have you believe that God does not want you to be creative? Or that if you go after God and do things His way, you will be stifled in your creativity and you will never make it?

Reflectors of Him

God desires that His Glory will be made manifest in and through you as a reflector of Him on the earth. It has always been His desire to show up in beauty, power and holiness, yet the challenge for men and women of all generations has been to yield to His Spirit and His Way.

"And it shall come to pass in the last days, that the mountain of the LORD's house shall be established in the top of the mountains, and shall be exalted above the hills; and all nations shall flow unto it.

"And many people shall go and say, Come ye, and let us go up to the mountain of the LORD, to the house of the God of Jacob; and he will teach us of his ways, and we will walk in his paths: for out of Zion shall go forth the law, and the word of the LORD from Jerusalem." - Isaiah 2:2-3 (KJV)

God desires to establish His dwelling among His people. He wants to be with us and to teach us His ways but there are many obstacles, one of which deals specifically with artists. *"Their land also is full of idols; they worship the work of their own hands, that which their own fingers have made"* (vv 8; emphasis added).

The Strategy of the Enemy

The sin of the Israelites, Lucifer, Cain and even us today is that instead of enjoying the habitation of the Lord in our midst and finding our identity from Him, we create idols – works of our own hands – that we want to elevate above God so that we could be exalted and affirmed. This has been the plan of the enemy from the beginning, to ensnare and enslave us through fear, pride and isolation.

1. Fear

The enemy plants fear in your heart – sometimes in big doses, sometimes small – that you are the only one who is able to look out for yourself. He tells you that everyone else in the world, including God, is out to take advantage of you. Using difficult circumstances in your own experience where you might not have felt affirmed, loved or accepted, the enemy replays the lie over and over again: *"See, I told you they didn't really love you, don't let that happen again!"*

Early in my teenage years, I felt that if people knew the real me; the me that had been sexually abused, the me that was confused about my own identity, the me that loved God and yet lived a secret life, they would push me away and I would be abandoned. A good friend of mine once told me that FEAR means "False Expectations Appearing Real." Most of the time the expectation of what might happen is worse than what is actually possible.

2. Pride

In the same way the enemy uses lies to build fear, he will exploit pride, immaturity and arrogance in our hearts to build a view of our work and ourselves based on a false sense of self-importance. During this process the enemy whispers lies, even in times of great joy and accomplishment, saying *"You really are the most talented person in the class"* or *"I am glad they finally recognize your gifting and that you are getting the praise you deserve."* The enemy will even arrange opportunities for you to be around people that feed the pride and selfish ambition in your life, further establishing the lies that you are the center of the creative universe.

Over the years I have watched this dynamic in the lives of many musicians and artists. One in particular was a guy I knew years ago who played lead guitar. He was an amazing musician, songwriter and worship leader. The downside was that he was very immature in his character while in a high-profile leadership role. I watched him over the years deal with issues of pride, especially as it concerned his congregation's openness to him doing original music. It not only became a source of contention in the churches he served, but the enemy used it in the entire worship team. Instead of encouraging the team to serve the congregation with the gifting they had been given, there arose an "us against them" mentality on the team as they sought to protect their leader.

The core issue the enemy used in this man was pride in his own anointing. *"Don't they know that God is giving me these songs? How dare they quench what God is doing in my ministry! We are not going to let them stop the flow of the Spirit; we just have to go after God!"* The real danger was that the worship team was snared in the trap as they encouraged him to go for it. The power and destruction of pride often affects far more than just the person at the center. It can draw and deceive others into a dangerous web as well.

3. Isolation
Once fear and pride begin to operate in your life, they create an unholy alliance that draws you deeper into a dark hole. How

many artists and creative people do you know who are loners or who struggle with depression?

The reason many artists are depressed is that they believe no one else understands them; everyone is out to use them so it is simply better to be alone. Why would they want to be around other people, especially artists? Someone might try to steal their ideas or copy their work. It is a never-ending cycle of lies. Once they are alone, it is debilitating and the creative spark they once enjoyed is in danger of being extinguished amid fear, anxiety and loneliness.

I know countless artists who struggle with isolation. They are so bound up in fear that it is just easier for them to be alone than to press into relationships. One such artist that comes to my mind is a woman I have known for many years. She is an extremely gifted painter yet she has to be begged to come out of the house to be around anyone. When she does come out, she avoids relationships because she is bound by fear that someone might see her work and take advantage of her gifting. It is a sad situation because the Father desires so much more for her!

God's Strategy for Success

The Father has a better way that is the opposite of how the enemy operates. His way is grounded in three basic Kingdom truths: Faith, Humility and Community.

1. Faith

The Bible says that without faith it is impossible to please God (Hebrews 11:6). Faith is the opposite of fear. It is the ultimate trust in God grounded in His goodness through Jesus and empowered by the Holy Spirit. When you begin to operate in faith, fear has to leave. Faith brings light and fear brings darkness. When the Light comes, the darkness has to flee.

What does faith look like in your life as an artist? Faith declares that your creativity, talent and gifting all come from the Father, are rooted in the Father and are of no enduring value outside of the inspiration of the Holy Spirit. Faith is a posture of leaning upon the breast of your Beloved (Song of Solomon 8:5) as you listen to His heart and reflect His Glory to the earth. With faith operating in your life, creative expression comes alive to create real beauty for the pleasure of the Lord and people.

Faith understands that God has called you to co-labor with Him in the Kingdom. It is a realization that everything He has endowed you with is for a divine purpose. The Father wants you to be inspired by the Holy Spirit so that the person you were created to be shines through in the light of His grace. He created you with specific design features that are required in order for you to fulfill your calling on the earth.

2. Humility
When you rightly understand yourself and who you are in Christ, you can truly walk in your calling as an artist. The model Jesus gives in the Bible is not one of some lame-o pansy that let everyone run over Him in the name of being humble. In fact, it is quite the opposite. Like Jesus, your testimony is to be one of strength, centered on Him and focused on walking in the authority He has given you. You are only able to follow Jesus' model when you do it the way He did.

Jesus knew who He was – the Son of God; what He was called to do – usher in the Kingdom; and how He was to accomplish His calling – by only doing what He saw the Father do and speaking what He heard the Father say. There is no opportunity for pride in that model as it is all about dependence on the Father. Your strength and authority are perfected in that dependence on God as joint heirs with Jesus and co-laborers with Him in the Kingdom.

Pride is simply a self-protecting mechanism created to mask our true fear of not being good enough. We bloat our outward self in order to feel good on the inside. When we understand who we are in Christ, pride falls to the side. We no longer have to prove ourselves, exalt ourselves or protect ourselves from those whom we have feared in the past. Instead, we are able to enter into His rest and our true identity in Him.

3. Community

God's plan is that you walk in wholeness with those around you. Real, vital, encouraging, life-giving relationships are His desire for your life! One thing that is vital about community, especially as it relates to artists, is that it must be intentional. Unless you purpose in your life to reach out to others in relationship for encouragement, support and collaboration, the enemy will work overtime to keep you isolated. For most wanting vulnerable and transparent relationships is not something that comes naturally but as you pursue them, the Father promises to reward you!

The Father encourages us to have "running buddies" to live life with:

"There was a man all alone;
he had neither son nor brother.
There was no end to his toil,
yet his eyes were not content with his wealth.
'For whom am I toiling,' he asked,
'and why am I depriving myself of enjoyment?'
This too is meaningless—
a miserable business!
Two are better than one,
because they have a good return for their work:
If one falls down,
his friend can help him up.
But pity the man who falls

and has no one to help him up!
Also, if two lie down together, they will keep warm.
But how can one keep warm alone?
Though one may be overpowered,
two can defend themselves.
A cord of three strands is not quickly broken." - Ecclesiastes 4:8-12 (NIV)

Isn't that encouraging? God gives you friends, who are there to help you when you fall, keep you warm when you are cold and defend you when you are attacked. God's design for your life in the Kingdom is one that is lived in authentic, loving community.

I encourage you today to press in to this journey with a posture of faith, humility and desire for community. Choose today to focus your worship and creative energy on the creator and His reality, not just the work of your hands. He's waiting for you!

Journal and Discussion Questions

1. *Do you struggle with pride in your artistic works? Take a moment to describe your own journey as an artist in the Kingdom?*

2. *Do you relate to Lucifer's desire to see himself exalted, rather than submitting himself to God's plan and authority for his life? Take a moment to explore this within yourself.*

3. *Have you ever experienced the cycle of Fear, Pride and Isolation in your life? Take a moment to process your own feelings and experiences here.*

4. *How do you feel about co-laboring with Christ in the Kingdom as a joint-heir with Him?*

5. *Do you have patterns of pride and self-protection in your life? Stop right now and ask the Lord to show you. Once He does, write down what you see and hear. He wants to heal you and give you the gift of humility.*

Chapter 14

Close the Gate: The Artist, Temptation & Habitual Sin

It was as if I was no longer a Christian. How could I continue to be bound in sin and habitual failure when I confessed Jesus as Lord, went to church, fellowshipped with other believers, prayed for the infilling of the Holy Spirit and was even in ministry? How was it that the worship songs that I wrote, the times I would lead others into the presence of God and the works of ministry I would perform could be so power-filled and yet I felt so empty and defeated?

For many years, this was my story. I was a husband, artist and uber-creative worship leader who loved ministry, my family and the presence of God. Yet, on a daily basis, I was yielding to patterns of habitual sin in my life. It was as if everything I did on Sunday mornings and even in my quiet times before the Lord meant nothing – at least that is the way I felt.

Because artists are so in tune with our feelings, we are especially susceptible to unhealthy patterns of sin in our life. I mean really, how many artists have you known or heard of who are alcoholics, drug addicts, performance junkies, egomaniacs, depressed, suicidal, sexual addicts, etc. It is the wounded pattern of Cain that we talked about earlier in the chapter on our lineage as artists. Unless we allow the Holy Spirit to restore and redeem our hearts and creative pursuits, we will continue to exist as immature believers, ruled by our emotions, led by feelings of woundedness and hounded by feelings of worthlessness, shame and fear.

Common Struggles

I have come to understand that this struggle is not common only to me, but is shared by countless artists and creative people. The very attributes God imparted into our DNA – sensitivity, creativity, ability to hear his voice, desire for adventure, love of excitement, love for beauty – are the doors Satan will use in our life to trap us if we are not mindful of his schemes and devices. It has often been said "Satan will attack you in your greatest area of weakness and if unsuccessful, your greatest area of strength.". Even the Apostle Paul lamented the fact that he often did the things he did not want to do and struggled to do the things he wanted to do.

As a person who believes in the healing power of God and His desire to manifest His healing in our lives today, I often wondered why God would not just heal me. Quite frankly, I had a lot of shame around this issue. I wondered why God would deliver others and not me. What was so wrong with me that I was not able to garner God's favor in my situation? My struggle was mostly based in pornography, lack of trust, fear of intimacy, performance and other woundedness that came out of being sexually molested as a young teen. It was indeed my way of coping with life and but at the same time 100% sin. Pretty soon, my sinful patterns were the only solution I found to any problem I faced. Feeling stress? Look at porn. Feeling happy? Look at porn. Feeling alone, sad? Need to celebrate? The pattern for me was the same: do not trust, fear the worst, hide in isolation and self-medicate. My learned reaction over the years was that in order to feel better, I should go back to the sin patterns I knew most intimately. I now know that our brain actually creates real patterns of electrical activity when we perform certain actions.

Not only do you become familiar with acting in a certain way, but your brains actually create an electrical groove to follow when specific emotions are felt.

The good news is our Father has a better way! He's designed you with your sensitivities for a very unique purpose in the earth. At the same time, He offers real solutions for walking in victory over temptation and habitual sin. In my own journey toward healing and wholeness I've been both frustrated and encouraged by one simple fact: God loves me too much just to do a quick work – zap! He is all about walking with you on the journey of wholeness, forgiveness, community and healing so that the things He works in your heart are rooted deep – for the long term – producing much fruit in your life. He can indeed heal your mind and help you create new, healthy patterns of dealing with frustrations, so that your actions are life-producing, not death-producing. The Father wants to see you free from every chain that hinders your abundant life in Him. It's His good pleasure to give you good gifts – including freedom!

Close the Gate

One day, when I was lamenting this struggle and asking the Lord "Why, why, why? Why do I continue to struggle like this?" the Lord said something profound to me. He said "You're leaving the gate open. Just close the gate." Immediately my heart said "Yes, that makes total sense!". If I did not want the enemy to enter into certain areas of my life, I needed to close the gate. Then He showed me that I had several gates – eyes, ears, mind, heart and body – and in order to keep myself safe, I needed to close those gates to the enemy. Here is a great example from my own life.

A big open gate I had was unfiltered Internet usage. I never had an internet monitoring filter on my computers at home and work. The result was unfettered access between me and my greatest struggle – online pornography and chatting. At any time I could log on, view sites I should not or chat online and erase my tracks without anyone knowing. Believe me, it was a huge snowball that was rolling downhill fast. The solution? I got filtered internet access on all my computers (home and work) that recorded my every track on the internet and reported it to 3 of my closest accountability partners. Not only that, it blocked sites I should not go to and told my friends I had tried to get there. I cannot uninstall it without their permission and it will even send them text messages if I try to hack the system. Literally for like $40 and a little willpower, I closed a major gate in my life. The effect of closing that one gate has been overwhelming. Instead of immediately going to that old pattern of sin, I have to stop and say – nope, that gate is closed and I need to find another way. It is in that split second that the Holy Spirit will open another gate for me to walk through.

For others, open gates in your life may include angry outbursts, manipulating people or situations in your life, substance abuse or even the temptation to always 'be on stage' when in reality you just want people to accept you for who you really are on the inside. Whatever the gate is I believe the Lord wants to help you close the unhealthy, dangerous gates in your life and open healthy, safe gates in your life that will feed and fulfill your spirit instead of bringing fear, shame and death.

Steps to Freedom

Let me offer the following steps to closing unhealthy gates in your own life, so you can get on with mining all the richness God has for your life and creative expression!

1) **Identify the Triggers & Gates In Your Life.** Through prayer, meditation on God's Word and interaction with people you love and trust, the Lord will reveal to you the specific triggers,

sin patterns and gates in your life that need to be addressed. By trigger I mean something that sets you off in the direction of your habitual sin pattern.

For example, you might experience stress, which leads to anger, which leads to you taking a drink, which leads to 5 drinks and you eventually passing out. Another example might be performance oriented. You might struggle with a low self-image and so to compensate, you put on a big, vivacious personality to cover your weakness. You are always on the offense, and in control of all your relationships. The minute that someone criticizes your or you feel out of control, you burst into anger, attacking those around you.

You may have one or like me, several. Just ask the Lord to reveal these to your heart. He will never reveal to you more than you can work through at one time. Remember, His goal is not to shame you but rather to see you walk in wholeness and vitality!

2) **Repent & Be Cleansed.** Once the Lord reveals areas of habitual sin and, brokenness in your life, it is important to come out of agreement with those actions and belief patterns. You may have already begun to work on these issues in the chapter on "Removing the Roadblocks". Repent (turn) and ask the Lord to forgive you for patterns of sin, unbelief, and agreement with the enemy. Then take a moment and ask the Father to wash you with the blood of Jesus, so that every stain, remnant and old pattern is removed.

3) **Confess Your Sins & Be Healed.** In James 5:16, the Bible teaches "Confess your sins to each other that you may be healed." This is an important truth for you to understand: true healing is worked out in the context of community, not as a lone ranger. There are some things in your life that are so

deeply engrained with you that without the Spirit-led help of others, you will never get over them. The enemy has always worked in isolation, loneliness and fear. Frankly, if you're like me, you may have even enjoyed staying in your own private pity party. It's easier sometimes to be wounded alone than to be healed in community, at least in the short-term. When you are alone and isolated, no one knows the 'real you' – or at least that's what you think. The truth is that God's design for your wholeness is based in the Body of Christ. There are some things tied to your healing, calling and destiny that you will never experience unless you are in real, authentic community with others.

One word of warning: you need to make sure that the people you are in relationship with are safe, especially when it comes to walking through brokenness and confessing sin. By 'safe' I mean people who value the same things you do, who will observe a high level of confidentiality, who you respect and who you can be honest with. Otherwise, you are setting yourself up for major disappointment. In my own life, there are very few people I have this type of relationship with, and I would say that is a good thing. God is not asking you to air your dirty laundry in front of everyone, but He is asking you to live in real community with a nucleus of people who really know you – all of you.

4) **Close the Gates.** Now that you have identified, repented from and confessed areas of habitual sin or strongholds in your life, take action to close the open gates that remain. Again, this is an area where it is helpful to walk in community. You probably do not see all the areas of vulnerability in your own life like your core group of friends do. Ask those safe people in your life to help you identify the open gates and develop real ways to close them.

If you struggle with socially based triggers, it may be that you cannot be in relationship with some people anymore or at least for a season. I had one such relationship in my life. This friend was like my alter ego. Every time we would get together I would talk, act and think in ways that I never would normally. It was not that this person was necessarily a horrible person, they just brought out the worst in me – lust, greed, manipulation, etc. I had to cut off that relationship for a season while God healed me and them.

5) **Develop New Pathways.** Once you have decided to close a gate in your life, it is extremely important to develop new, healthy pathways. Without new pathways, it is very easy to return to old patterns. Developing new pathways is best done in the context of vulnerable, authentic, safe relationships. For me, I had no clue how to develop healthy patterns of dealing with stress or loneliness, because I had operated in an unhealthy way for so long. I had to become intentional about developing some alternatives and many of the tools I now use came from friends who love me.

One of the new pathways I have developed is not to travel alone. For me, doing so just brings up too many dangerous feelings. I now travel with my wife or a safe friend if possible or if I have to actually travel by myself, I stay with safe friends at my destination and let my wife know where I am at the whole time. Why do I want to travel, get a rental car, eat alone and stay in a hotel room by myself when I know that would be a major trigger for me? That is just stupid. Part of growing up and taking the 'big boy pill' is taking responsibility for my life and actions – weaknesses and all. Honestly, there is a lot of freedom that comes in that!

Through the power of the Spirit, the foundation of His Word and your investment in healthy Christian community, you can close the gates to habitual patterns of sin in your life!

Journal and Discussion Questions

1. *Have you ever dealt with feelings of worthlessness, shame or fear? Take a moment to talk about your struggle here.*

2. *What do you really believe about God's desire for your freedom? For example, do you believe that He CAN heal you but doesn't WANT to heal you? Explain.*

3. *Take a moment to identify the triggers and open gates in your life. Ask the Holy Spirit to bring light to the situation and reveal truth to your heart.*

4. *Who are the 'safe' people in your life? What's your plan to engage them in real accountability in your life?*

5. *What are the new pathways that the Lord is revealing to you? Take a moment to list them below and then share these with your 'safe' people.*

Chapter 15

Turn Your Heart: Raising Up the Next Generation

By now, I pray God has imparted great vision in your heart for your calling in His Kingdom as an artist! There is such great possibility and potential that lay ahead for you, but as leadership guru John Maxwell says "There is no success without a successor." Even greater still is the dynamic of the Kingdom of God based on spiritual fathering and mothering. You are commanded raise up the next generation and as Malachi 4:6 says, allow the Father to "turn our hearts".

> *"And he shall turn the heart of the fathers to the children, and the heart of the children to their fathers, lest I come and smite the earth with a curse."*

Without intentionally turning your hearts to the next generation, the generation of emerging artists around you, you may never realize the full impact of your calling in the Kingdom. Not only that, the generation that comes behind you will start out in a place of weakness, not strength, having to aimlessly navigate through land you have already taken.

Throughout the Bible, you can see incredible examples of how God's people intentionally reached back and pulled forward into their calling those around them. Bezalel had Oholiab as his apprentice. Moses had Joshua. Asaph, Jeduthan and Heman had all the tabernacle musicians and prophets they led and mentored them. The prophet Elijah had his protégé Elisha. Jesus had the 12 disciples. Paul had Timothy. There is something powerful that happens when you raise up another person into their calling. It is the way God has designed life to be released and maturity to come forth in the Kingdom, especially for artists.

Life-Givers

As a spiritual father or mother, you are not called to make everyone look like, act like and talk like you. In fact, the opposite is true. The word 'father' means 'life giver'. You are to impart the life of God to those He places around you. Your role is simply to love them, hear the Lord with them, challenge them, stretch them and call forth the purpose that God's placed on their life. You should never want to make 'mini-me's' out of them but pray that God would allow you to see their unique purpose and calling emerge.

Real spiritual fathers are uncommon. In fact, even Paul wrote in 1 Corinthians 4:15:

> *"For though you might have ten thousand instructors in Christ, yet you do not have many fathers; for in Christ Jesus I have begotten you through the gospel."*

So what is the difference, you may ask, between what Paul calls "instructors" and what God is calling us to as spiritual fathers and mothers. I have put together a comparison chart for you to consider below. All though it is not a comprehensive list by any means, hopefully you begin to understand the differences God wants to highlight among us.

Attributes of Teachers

- Conveys information
- Disciplines to keep order
- Teaches out of books & other resources
- Keeps professional distance
- Passes or fails their students
- Are there for a season
- Walk proudly
- Authority is based on position
- Instructs students to keep the rules

Attributes of Fathers

- Imparts truth based on their life experience
- Disciplines to bring maturity
- Teaches based on experience & scars
- Develops close relationships that go beyond the surface
- Loves unconditionally in success or failure
- Are there for a lifetime
- Walk with a "limp"
- Authority is based on Godly influence
- Invites you to follow as they follow Christ

From Instructor to Teacher

The first time I was asked to be a spiritual father to someone, I was totally unprepared and messed it up pretty badly. Because of my own unresolved woundedness stemming from the father issues I had as a boy, I was unable to father this young man in a way that was pleasing to the Father. In fact, it was pretty horrible.

First of all, I was jealous. This guy was incredibly talented, good looking and well connected within the church. As long as everyone knew he was 'my assistant' I was great but as soon as they started asking for him to lead a song during worship, it was all over. Honestly, I was crazed in my head. I had always been the one everyone loved. Now, this young guy I had been entrusted to raise up was, in my mind, stealing the spotlight. Because of my own "stuff", I worked to sabotage the relationship. We have since reconciled, thank God, but it was a rough couple of years there, for sure.

I was very comfortable in the role of teacher: do what I say, follow the rules, don't screw up, make me look good and everything will go well for you. But God was calling me to be more than just a mere instructor. He was calling me to invest myself in this young man, show him my scars, lead by example, reach into his heart and pull for the calling of God on his life. Out of self-protection I chose not to.

God's call to you is the same today. Will you ask the Father who He has placed in your circle of influence? Who is it that He has called you to invest your life in, to pour your knowledge in and to impart your wisdom to? I encourage you to ask the Father to begin opening up those doors for you so you can start pouring out life to those around you and seeing the Kingdom advance! Our ceiling should be the floor for the next generation.

Practical Steps to Spiritually Fathering Emerging Artists

Based on the attributes of fathers I listed above, I would like to offer you a blueprint of how to walk in healthy relationship with those God calls you to father in the Spirit.

Impart Truth based on Your Life Experience

As you reach out to emerging artists around you, do not feel like you have it all together and project some image of perfection. That only sets you up for failure and them up for disappointment. Instead, as you build relationship with them, ask the Lord to highlight experiences you have had and truths you have learned on your journey. When you speak from there, you have authority to impart the truth the Father has worked in you.

Discipline to Bring Maturity

One of the traits I see in healthy fathers and mothers is that the core of their desire focuses in the maturity of their child. If you have to bring correction to someone your working with, whether it is in a spiritual, relational or purely artistic endeavor, I would encourage you to do it in private. I heard someone say once "Praise in public, correct in private." That is a great model for us as ones called to raise up others in their calling. Our desire should never to be to embarrass or 'call on the carpet'. Rather, ask the Lord how to approach the matter with love, patience and insight from the Spirit of God.

Teach Based on Experience & Scars

The places in my life where I fell the hardest are the places I have the most authority now. For me, the biggest wounds in my life were in the realm of purity, fathering and identity. As you walk in freedom from the things that have held you bound in your own life, you will carry a larger amount of authority in to be able to bring others into freedom as well. However, it is not all about your woundedness. There are places in your life where you have a large amount of freedom and authority already. Teach from the places of strength as well – just do not hide your flaws. Jesus calls us to walk as He walked, as what renown theologian Henri Nouwn called a "wounded healer".

Develop Close Relationships that Go Beyond the Surface

Theodore Roosevelt said, "People don't care how much you know until they know how much you care." It has become cliché but how true it is! If you are the one that God has called as the spiritual father or mother in the relationship, then it is incumbent on you to reach out and foster the relationship with the one you are called to walk with. Take them out for dinner, invite them over for a movie, take time together in the studio for collaboration, talk about topics other than 'work' or 'art'. God is calling you to invest in their life, not just teach them skills.

Love Unconditionally in Success or Failure

When working with people we will always experience failure or what we perceive as failure. Maybe they did not do it the way you asked them to, or just failed all together. It is important in any relationship that people know you love them and that your love isn't changing based on their ability or inability to perform. People are longing to know you love them and that you see God's potential in their life, beyond their current circumstances. The worst thing you can do in raising up the next generation is to place them on some sort of performance track. Keep the standards high, but at the same time keep the relationships strong! Major on love.

Are There for a Lifetime

I believe true spiritual fathers and mothers are not just there today and gone tomorrow. You cannot just lead someone to the Lord, walk away and call yourself a spiritual parent to them. The words 'father' and 'mother' imply family, as in ones who are there through thick and thin; ones who continually lead and guide. I pray that the people you choose to invest your life in are ones you can walk with for many years. I'm privileged to be on staff at a church where one of my spiritual fathers is on staff. It is a joy to know that after many years of relationship, we are still walking the Kingdom together. I can at any time walk in his office, close the door and get some much needed perspective! That is priceless.

Recently, I heard of a spiritual father in the faith who made a comment to one of his spiritual sons, saying "You can have as much of me as you want." That is the kind of spiritual parenting you and I need: fathers and mothers that will love their sons and daughters unto life.

Walk with a Limp

So many heroes of the faith, including King David walked with a noticeable 'limp' after walking through brokenness. For most of us, it is part of walking life's journey. The difficulty becomes trying to hide the limp in your stride. I want to encourage you to own your limp. To a large extent, the brokenness you have experienced has made an indelible imprint on your life and expression of your creativity. Walk proudly but never allow it to define you! You are more than a sum total of your mistakes!

Authority based on Influence & Trust

Author and leadership guru John Maxwell draws a clear distinction between positional leaders versus leaders of influence in a recent *BusinessWeek* article on BusinessWeek.com. Maxwell says:

> *"Good leaders don't rely on their position, power, or title to do their work for them. They know leadership is about connecting with people."*[11]

If you have to constantly remind people that you are 'in charge', guess what? You are not. Leadership is about influencing others around you based in integrity, trust &

---

[11] Maxwell, John C. "Positional Leaders. Destined to Disappoint." *BusinessWeek – Business News, Stock Market & Financial Advice*. 12 July 2007. Web. 16 February 2011

respect. The more those characteristics are exhibited in your life as a leader, the more authority others will attribute to you.

Invite you to follow as they follow Christ

In 1 Corinthians 11:1, Paul exhorts the Corinthian church to *"Follow my example, as I follow the example of Christ."* That is really what raising up the next generation is all about. As you walk the journey of faith and creative expression in integrity, the Father asks you to turn and ask others to walk with you, imitating your every move. It is a big responsibility, but it is the way of the Kingdom!

Honoring the Fathers & Mothers

No matter your age or experience, you have a responsibility and calling from the Lord to not only reach backward to raise up, but to reach forward to honor the generation that has gone before you. The Bible instructs us in Exodus 20:21:

> *"Honor your father and your mother, that your days may be long upon the land which the LORD your God is giving you."*

Just like in Malachi 4, you see God's promise of life and favor when there's a turning of the heart toward honor. Honoring the fathers and mothers that have gone before you and paved the way in the Spirit is pivotal in reaching your full potential as an artist in the Kingdom.

That Your Days May Be Long in the Land

God has an incredible future for you in His Kingdom! According to Jeremiah 29:11, God reminds us, saying:

> *"For I know the plans I have for you,"* declares the LORD, *"plans to prosper you and not to harm you, plans to give you hope and a future."*

God's promise of long life in the land (your calling – your appointed place in the Kingdom) that He is giving you is tied to honoring your elders – the mothers and fathers in your life who have gone before you, prepared the way and created the platform of anointing and creativity on which you now stand!

God never designed us to have to rebuild the foundation of life and ministry in every generation! Rather, His perfect design is tied up in generational blessing, honor and impartation where the older generation raises up the younger – then the younger reach back, honor the older and stand on their shoulders! Anything less is allowing the enemy to rob your creative birthright!

Who are the spiritual mothers and fathers in your life? Ask the Lord to give you new passion to invest in those relationships and glean all He has for you through the elders He's placed in your life! I pray right now that God would release new desire and passion in your heart to honor the generation that has gone before you! I pray that as you honor them, the Spirit of God would capture your heart to turn and likewise raise up the spiritual children God calls into your life! May the generational blessing be your testimony as you help raise up this army of artists to show forth God's Glory in the earth!

Journal and Discussion Questions

1. *Who are the spiritual mothers and fathers in your life who have been 'life-givers' to your creative expression?*

2. *Do you naturally display the attributes of a Teacher or a Father, as described in this chapter?*

3. *As you move into maturity as one called to raise up the next generation, where do you most struggle? Authenticity? Transparency? Discipline? Real Relationship? Unconditional love?*

4. *Who are the ones God has placed in your circle of influence to mentor and raise up? What are you doing to actively walk with them in their journey?*

5. *Who are the ones God has placed in your life as mothers or fathers in this season to lean upon for strength and encouragement? What are you doing to actively walk with them in your journey?*

Appendix #1
The Leader's Guide

Unlocking the Heart of the Artist was initially written as a small group experience for the artists of The Worship Studio community in Canton, GA to have a resource to gather around, work through together and use as a springboard for deeper conversation, creative community and personal ministry. To that end, I have included Journal & Discuss Questions at the end of each chapter of the book. While there is no perfect way to facilitate this book as a small group, I would like to offer the following format as a starting point. It's born much fruit for us and I pray it will be a source of life for your group as well.

Timeframe: 2 hours sessions over a period of 12 -15 Weeks

Location: A creative, inspiring and intimate space conducive to worship, discussion and ministry.

Sample Meeting Schedule:

6:00 pm   **Meet & Greet**
Ever met an artist that was on time? Me either. Use this 'gathering time' for sharing recent projects, fellowship and catching up with each other.

6:15 pm   **Group Worship & Prayer**

This is a great time to let emerging worshippers take the reins and lead the group in worship and prayer.   Most of the time, acoustic worship (guitars, djembe's, keyboard, etc) work great in a small group atmosphere. If you need to use CD's, do it!

6:40 pm   **Check-In & Testimony**

Go around the room and ask for testimonies of what God has been speaking to them during the past week regarding the most recent chapter, their journaling, creative date or other applicable experiences. Celebrate breakthroughs and support each other in challenging situations. This is not a time to counsel or give advice – just listen.

This is a great time to incorporate a brief testimony from an artist each week focused on their creative journey so far, walk with the Lord, why they are participating in the group and what they hope to get out of it. I always encourage artists who are giving testimonies to bring an example of their work to share with the group.

7:00 pm   **The Lesson**

The facilitator should give a brief overview of the chapter, using the section headings as an easy springboard.   Of course, everyone has thoroughly read each chapter, but just in case there's the lone slacker, make sure everyone is on the same page.

Allow ample time for discussion of the topic along with personal testimonies in order to engage each group   member.   Encourage   everyone's participation and watch out for those who may want to either dominate or fade away into the background.

7:45 pm   **Prayer & Personal Ministry**

The most meaningful time of every meeting will be your time of prayer and personal ministry toward each other. Typically, the Lord will spotlight issues in every person's heart. I have often used the concept of a 'hot seat' in the middle of the room, where the person or people wanting prayer can sit, allowing everyone else to gather around and lay hands on them.

Let the Holy Spirit lead you during these special times. It's a great time to encourage participants to actively listen for the voice of the Holy Spirit and to encourage one another in the Lord with scripture and encouraging words from the Lord.

A "Weekend Away"

There's something about just getting away from the day-to-day routine of life and experiencing the solitude and refreshment that only a spiritual retreat can offer. One of the best ways to enable your creative community to grow together in the context of The Unlocking the Heart of the Artist Series is to do a "Weekend Away". Choose a place that's comfortable, refreshing, quite and conducive to the format you feel is best.

By all means, let the Holy Spirit lead you as you plan your weekend away. Make it special and a weekend to remember. Don't over plan. Leave room to 'breathe'. Some pieces I've found to be life-giving over the years are:

- Group Worship
- Solo Experiences for Meditation & Creativity
- Teaching & Discussion Sessions
- Visual Journaling
- Campfires, Nature Hikes, Labyrinth Prayers
- Times of Individual Affirmation from the Group
- Drag & Brag – allowing artists to bring recent work and share
- Campfires, S'mores and Singalongs

Note: Each year, The Worship Studio sponsors an "Unlocking the Heart of the Artist" retreat that is open to artists of every medium. In addition, Matt Tommey and other Worship Studio team members are available to speak at retreats in your local area. For more information, visit www.theworshipstudio.org.

Appendix #2
The Vision of The Worship Studio

Statement of Community Need

The community of artists and creative people around the world have been largely disenfranchised by the Church because they don't easily 'fit the mold' of what current religious systems deem appropriate. Artists think outside the box, push back on traditional social and religious ideology and are often seen as threats to the status quo. Instead of the church and the creative community being a mutual source of life, they have largely ignored one another.

The institutional church has gone on with business as usual while many artists are walking in brokenness, jettisoned from the life-giving source Christ offered through authentic Christian community. Because they have little context by which to experience Christ in their creativity and yet desire a deeper purpose in their work, many artists pursue new age spiritualism, paganism, atheism or art for art's sake – leaving them more empty and confused.

We believe that God created creative people in His very image and wants to use them significantly in society to shift culture & reveal His Glory in the earth. We believe the very creative DNA of

God resides in artists and that the Father wants nothing less than to redeem and restore them to Himself. This redemption and restoration process requires that we raise up artists in authentic community who are walking in wholeness, know how to hear the voice of the Lord and engage the Holy Spirit in their creative expression while operating at a high skill level

How It Started

During a season of crying out the Lord for revelation about my calling and my place in the Kingdom, the Father woke me up 2 mornings in a row at around 3:09 am -3:10 am. The song that was playing in my head was a song by Jason Upton called "Lion of Judah" where it says "Raise up an army, raise up an army, raise up an army like Joel saw!" On the second morning, I went to my studio and opened up the Bible to Joel 3:09 (NLT) and sure enough, here is what it said:

> "Say to the nations far and wide:
> 'Get ready for war!
> Call out your best warriors.
> Let all your fighting men advance for the attack.
> Hammer your plowshares into swords
> and your pruning hooks into spears.
> Train even your weaklings to be warriors.
> Come quickly, all you nations everywhere.
> Gather together in the valley.'
> And now, O Lord, call out your warriors!

> "'Let the nations be called to arms.
> Let them march to the valley of Jehoshaphat.
> There I, the Lord, will sit
> to pronounce judgment on them all.
> Swing the sickle,
> for the harvest is ripe.

Come, tread the grapes,
for the winepress is full.
The storage vats are overflowing
with the wickedness of these people.'"

The Lord told me I was to go to the nations, gather the warriors and the weaklings – the master artists and the emerging artists – and raise up an army of artists to reveal His Glory in the earth. He showed me how in this passage of scripture, warriors and those that saw themselves as weak were being called together to take whatever was in their hands – the normal tools of their trade (plowshares & pruning hooks) – and turn them into instruments of war. The Father then showed me that this movement of artists was pivotal to His end-time purposes of bringing in the great harvest in our generation.

Camp Out by the River of God

The next morning, the Father woke me up again early. While I was praying, the Lord told me to go to Ezekiel 47 and I began to read about the Healing Waters and the River of God. In this passage the Lord describes how there are mighty trees planted by the water, how they yield fruit every month and how their leaves are for the healing of the nations. That's when the Lord told me that our job at The Worship Studio was to "camp out by the river of God". He said He would plant master artists like mighty oak trees in The Worship Studio and their shade would bring comfort and rest to emerging artists as they gathered around. Then I looked up and saw the wind blowing through the trees. The Lord told me that these master artists – mighty trees – would spawn many branches (artists) and fruit (art). He said "And every leaf will sing a little different, paint a little different, dance a little different as the wind of my Spirit blows through the trees. And the leaves will be used for the healing of the nations."

With these two clear mandates from the Lord, The Worship Studio was born. Since then, God has continued to clarify the vision and:

The Purpose of The Worship Studio Movement
The Worship Studio is:

- An Equipping Resource for Artists
- A Catalyst for Creativity in the Kingdom
- A Hub for Creative Communities

Our vision is to encourage and equip artists to form creative communities committed to fostering personal wholeness, engaging the Holy Spirit in their creative process, artistic skill development and releasing the Glory of God through creative expression.

The Strategy of The Worship Studio Movement
God has given us a 3-fold strategy for ministry in order to effectively lead artists into the fullness of what God has for their lives and creativity. The strategy includes: Wholeness, Prophecy & Creative Skill.

Wholeness
God desires for all people to walk in complete freedom and wholeness. Through loving community, relationships, healing ministry and accountability artists will come into a deeper measure of wholeness in their life.

> *"The thief does not come except to steal, and to kill, and to destroy. I have come that they may have life, and that they may have it more abundantly"* - John 10:10

Prophecy

As artists are coming into wholeness, we encourage them to hear and engage the Holy Spirit in order to understand His desire for their life and creative expression. Out of those encounters with the Lord, artists learn to respond to the voice of the Holy Spirit through their life and unique creative expression, revealing the Testimony of Jesus in the earth.

> *"For the testimony of Jesus is the spirit of prophecy."* - Revelation 19:10

Skill

In the spirit of Bezalel & Oholiab & the musicians in the Tabernacle of David, we encourate artists to minister skillfully before the Lord as they create and worship through creative expression. Through mentoring and training relationships with master artists, participation in learning opportunities and practice, we will train artists to become master artists within their chosen medium.

> *"See, I have chosen Bezalel son of Uri, the son of Hur, of the tribe of Judah, and I have filled him with the Spirit of God, with skill, ability and knowledge in all kinds of crafts- to make artistic designs for work in gold, silver and bronze, to cut and set stones, to work in wood, and to engage in all kinds of craftsmanship."* - Exodus 31:2-5

How Does It Look?

Our desire is to see creative communities established all over the world who share the same DNA, commitment and passion to raising up an army of artists to reveal the Glory of God in the earth as we do. God is mobilizing all of us for His purposes in our generation as we form this network of creative communities around the world. By design, every artist and consequently, every creative community will be a little different depending on the artists God uses to establish the community and their collective passion.

The first studio we formed, in Canton, Georgia (NW Metro Atlanta) is actually a working artist community with art classes, monthly worship opportunities, classes & workshops and more located in a physical building on 2 acres. Other communities that are springing up are simply groups of artists who gather at a local coffee shop or home to discuss their faith, art and life. The beauty of being a part of an artist community is that each community can be as unique as the artists involved. The sky is the limit!

We are currently working on the development of a creative community in Asheville that will serve as the headquarters for The Worship Studio, including worship, training with master artists, workshops, seminars, conferences and retreats, personal ministry and mentoring. Our dream is that God would raise up an epi-center – a prototype - of creativity and anointing that would be a deep well of blessing and healing for artists around the world.

What About You?

Are you passionate about seeing a creative community form in your local area? For more resources on forming a creative community in your local area, please visit http://www.theworshipstudio.org/about/communities

To be a part of The Worship Studio Community, we simply ask that you align your creative community with the values outlined on the website above, including:

- Our DNA for Ministry as described in our Vision & Strategy
- Offering the "Unlocking the Heart of the Artist" Series in your Community
- Fostering Creative Community Among Artists
- Collaboration & Support Among Communities

Appendix #3

There is a Non-Physical Reality

As you embrace your calling to reveal the very nature and person of Jesus in the earth through your creative expression, it's important to realize there's a very real, non-physical reality that the Father has given us to live, move and create within. We are not just physical beings and the world we live in is not just a physical world! We are spirit, soul and body, equipped to engage creatively with the Father on all levels.

For many years, a good friend of mine David Van Koevering has done much research in the field of quantum physics and it's relation to the spiritual truths of the Bible. The revelation he's received from the Father is especially poignant for ones called to create. I'd like to share some of his thoughts with you on the reality of the non-physical reality in which we live.

According to David Van Koevering. . .

"Years ago, as a young scientist and inventor, I worked with Dr. Bob Moog and together we gave the music world the first performance keyboards called Moog synthesizers. I learned to work with electrons and photons, tiny elements that are so small they can't be seen! Yet these invisible elements cause all electronic devices to work. This project caused me to ask the question, "Is there more to our universe than what I can perceive through my senses?"

My search to learn more about physical reality and how it works led me to discover that quantum physics identifies a large part of our universe to be non-physical. I began to realize that the universe is greater than science has discovered, or can explain. Through quantum physics and spiritual revelation, the Holy Spirit confirmed keys to understanding physical reality. As you read this book, allow the Holy Spirit to let you hear more than I say.

My studies in quantum mechanics led me to the works of Max Planck, Albert Einstein, Niels Bohr, and others. Here I learned that everything we see is part of a vast ocean of infinitesimally small subatomic particles. Under certain conditions, these subatomic structures also take on the properties of invisible waves. When I learned that these waves, or particles which make up all matter, cause that matter to blink into existence by being observed by the experimenter, I was shaken to my core.

How could it be that these invisible elements, which make up all matter, can be changed from particles to waves by how they are observed? This reality is beyond our human consciousness and our five senses. Or is it? All of these particles and/or waves appear to be connected. How can it be that every atomic and subatomic element is hooked up? Is this invisible world a part of the spiritual realm?

I suppose the duality of matter being waves or particles and how quantum mechanics attempts to explain this revolutionary idea changed me forever. It caused me to do my own research, which led to the convergence of quantum mechanics and my personal spiritual revelation. I was about to take a quantum leap!

1 Corinthians 1:28 says, *'God (has) chosen...things which are not (the invisible) to bring to nought things which are (the visible).'* This Scripture makes sense only when you understand it at the atomic and subatomic level. Everything is made up of atoms, which are frequencies of energy. These frequencies of energy are the voice of Jesus causing all things to be! Atoms are made up of subatomic particles, and subatomic particles are made up of superstrings (which are toroidal vortices of energy). Superstrings are tiny donut shaped packets of energy that spin at a frequency - or sing as in a pitch.

None of this is real in this dimension because they exist only in a state of possibilities until someone observes them. Then, at that observation, the potential becomes a thing - a particle or a wave. This quantum wave collapse, caused by observation, is called popping a qwiff. This is your first step to taking a quantum leap. You can see or observe a God qwiff (something God shows you that is not yet real in this dimension) and, by observing or popping that qwiff, cause that potential to become your reality. Be careful what you see; you are going to get it! Be careful what you say; you will get that, too!

Light is Slowing Down
The spiritual realm operates above the speed of light. The physical realm - this dimension - has been shaped to its current limits by the falls of both Lucifer (see Luke 10:18) and man in the Garden of Eden (see Genesis 3:7). When man fell, the speed of light slowed down. In the beginning, when God spoke the universe into existence, His entire bandwidth of glory was made physical. From His glory (all frequencies) and

His voice (all frequencies expressed) all light, energy, and matter became.

It is believed that the speed of light is 186,000 miles per second. Physicist Barry Setterfield, mathematician Trevor Norman, and Canadian mathematician Alan Montgomery have measured light and proven that the speed of light is slowing down.

That means that light may have been ten to thirty percent faster in the time of Christ; twice as fast in the days of Solomon; and four times as fast in the days of Abraham. My friend Chuck Missler says, 'That would imply that the velocity of light was more than ten million times faster prior to 3,000 B.C. This possibility would also alter our concepts of time and the age of the universe. The universe might actually be less than 10,000 years old!' That sounds like a quantum leap to me!

Before the fall, God had created one realm from gravity waves to His glory. This present human realm is up through the electromagnetic spectrum to the speed of light. The interesting point about the speed of light slowing down is that when Lucifer (the bearer of light) rebelled in Heaven and was cursed and cast down - and I believe cast down from the frequencies of God's glory - he lost his bandwidth and fell down from his spiritual consciousness. In the Garden of Eden, when mankind sinned, was cursed in the fall downward, and lost upper bandwidth and spiritual consciousness, light slowed down even more.

Other Biblical events suggest that the cosmos lost bandwidth. Noah's flood is such an example. Light slowed down to cause just the right frequencies for the rainbow (see Genesis 9:12-

17). At Nimrod's Tower of Babel, mankind lost the upper bandwidth to communicate (see Genesis 11:7).

Jesus Himself told His disciples that they will get their upper bandwidth back. In John 16:13 He said, *'when He, the Spirit of Truth, is come, He will guide you into all truth...and He will show you things to come.'* Jesus is saying, *'I want to show you your future. You can know My will and My plan for your life, although right now, you don't have the upper bandwidth to see or observe it. But when the Spirit of truth comes, He will give you the upper bandwidth to see things to come!'* This is the only source of your capacity!

Here is a quantum leap for someone: If you know something coming from your future, let's say a vision, a revelation, a desire, or even a creative idea, that information has to move faster than the speed of light to reach you. You can and must know your God-given assignment. Information flowing from your future possibilities is waiting for you to see - to observe - and call those things that are not as though they are. The quantum leap of knowing your purpose and assignment is waiting as a God qwiff for you to pop!

Matter is Frequency Being Spoken by Jesus
When God spoke and all the frequencies of His glory became manifest, the cosmos became! From the tiniest vibrating superstring that is causing or singing the atoms that make up the table of 103 elements, all the way through everything the Hubble telescope sees, are the vibrating frequencies of Jesus' voice.

Colossians 1:16-17 says, *'For by Him all things were created that are in Heaven and that are on earth, visible and invisible... He is before all things, and in Him all things consist (exist or are sustained).'* The phrase 'He is before all things' means that

He is outside of our time. Jesus said to John the Revelator that He was and is the Alpha (beginning) and Omega (ending). Jesus is outside our concept of time in His eternal now and is causing all things to be. Now the Periodic Table of Elements have been transposed into audio sounds. These sounds are Yahweh's voice calling matter to be!

When we consider creation and all things eternal, our false concepts regarding time and matter limit our understanding. Receive the concept that Jesus is outside of our time and calendar, looking in. He is observing. He is sustaining all things in this nanosecond (one billionth of a second) and is singing the frequencies or vibrations of your body. If He didn't, you would dissolve! Your electrons, particles, and subatomic structures are blinking in and out of existence. You think you are a solid object, but quantum mechanics has confirmed that all subatomic particles - the stuff you are made of - are blinking in and out of this reality.

Enoch was walking so closely with God in the Spirit that *'he was not, for God took him'* (see Genesis 5:24). Jesus simply stopped blinking Enoch into this realm! How close are you to Jesus Christ? How far away is your healing, your deliverance, or your miracle? He is close, for in Him you live and move and have your being.

In the next nanosecond, He sustains you or sings your frequency set. Understand that your healing or miracle is within the next nanosecond! In the blink of a nanosecond, He can cause your healing. Observe your healing, your miracle, your deliverance, and be filled with all Truth by observing the future God has for you. Take that quantum leap!

When we understand that we are being created in Christ by His causing, or by Him singing our song, our intimacy with Him will change. His song of creation was not something He did 16 billion years ago. He is causing you now! Because the speed of light has slowed down, because we have our upper bandwidth back, and because He is sustaining us every nanosecond, the act of creation is happening now! Take your quantum leap into His eternal now.

All Matter Has Memory. Your Words are Being Recorded

As a scientist and inventor, I have developed various memory retrieval systems. In the 1970s, I developed a laser optical music system to store sounds on silver oxide film and play the sounds back with keyboards, using modulated light beams. I was amazed when I found the Scripture in Joshua 24:27 (KJV) that says, 'And Joshua said unto all the people, *"Behold, this stone shall be a witness unto us; for it hath heard all the words of the LORD which He spake unto us: it shall be therefore a witness unto you, lest you deny your God."'*

Was this Old Testament quantum physicist saying that matter has memory? Is this man, who called for and observed the sun standing still in the heavens, telling us that the stone is listening? This is the man who sounded a frequency that cancelled the frequencies of matter in the walls of Jericho, thereby dissolving their atomic lattice structure with his shout and song. Did this man say the rocks are listening?

Jesus said the same thing. Joshua said the stone could record, and Jesus said in Luke 19:40 that the stones would cry out. Habakkuk 2:11 says, *'For the stone shall cry out of the wall, and the beam out of the timber shall answer it.'* I came to understand that all matter has memory. The Bible says that matter can record and it will play back. How can these things be?

As I studied both quantum theory and Scripture, revelation came. I learned that Gerald Feinberg, a physicist at Columbia University, named a certain subatomic particle, that he found in Einstein's math, after the Greek word tachys, meaning 'swift.' He called this superluminal particle a tachyon. This particle moved faster than light!

The tachyon is not looked upon favorably by physicists. If tachyons can be proven to exist and anything that moves faster than light can be found, scientists will have to explain how something can appear before its cause. For instance, if a scientific test was set up to look for this elusive faster-than-light tachyon, and the computer started at 12:00 noon counting forward through the test sequence, the test result wouldn't be at 12:01 or later. It would show the effect before the cause at 11:59 or earlier. Scientists don't have computers that count backwards and don't accept results that appear before the cause.

But wait. Two thirds of your Bible got to mankind before the event or cause! All prophecy is the result of facts before the event. All creativity comes before the actual physical reality! What is a vision? What is a word of knowledge? It is seeing, knowing, getting information before the causation. There is no other source of creativity than the Holy Spirit. All truth comes to man through the only source of truth we have, and that is the Holy Spirit. When you see your future, you are getting information faster than the speed of light through a means of streaming superluminal particles. The barrier of light speed is bridged from this subluminal realm to the higher bandwidth of the superluminal realm by the Holy Spirit.

Something like Gerald Feinberg's tachyon exists in all matter. It is just above, or faster than the speed of light. We know it's there because we find the results of such in the very fact of prophecy, or in the concept of words of knowledge, and even our Bible itself. These are proofs that the potential and possibilities of future promises or information is flowing to us. The superluminal tachyon-like connector exists!

That faster-than-light particle in all matter receives and remembers or records photons that shine on matter as in the photoelectric effect. Modulated photons go into all matter, reside in the vortex of superluminal faster-than-light particles, and knock electrons out. This photoelectric effect is how my modulated light musical instruments worked in the 1970s. That is how CD players and DVD players work now.

Today, it is not difficult to believe that matter has memory, because most of us have tiny memory sticks or memory cards that record or store information from our cameras and computers. Information flowing into matter and recalling it is commonplace. Photons from all light sources reflect from your body and off your belongings. Those information carrying photons go into all matter, including walls, your ring, and your watch. This information - even what we say and think - is modulating or moving through the connectedness of all atomic structures. This modulated photon goes in and electrons come out. That is why Joshua said, "This stone has heard." Every word, action, and deed done in the flesh has been recorded.

This is where yesterday went! It is all recorded in matter and will someday be played back. This is how evil and curses reside in places or things. Even though matter has recorded everything, your prayer in the name of Jesus can take the effect of Christ's blood - His blood that is eternal and beyond time - and cancel out all evil, sin, and past sin's memory from matter. Oh, that is a quantum leap for many! You can speak to and erase from places all curses and evil in Jesus' name.

Have you fixed your past? Have you removed all curses? Have you blessed the things you own? Have you blessed your house, office, car, belongings, money, computer, and phone? Are those things and places free from your past actions, words, and thoughts? You or someone else can speak a blessing or curse on your things. Somebody is about to take a quantum leap!

Seeing Your Future as God Sees it is Quantum Faith

Hebrews 11:1 says that faith is the substance. It is the invisible substance from which your physical world was and is being created by Jesus Christ. Annette Capps said, 'God used faith substance and word energy to create the universe. He spoke and the vibration (sound) of His words released (caused) the substance that became the stars and planets.'

God's future potential and all the promised possibilities constantly flow through the Holy Spirit into you. Noise on my circuit limits my ability to hear His voice and see His future for me. The noise in my inner man is not always sin; my noise can be my gift, my ability, even that special way I am put together and wired. I can become so busy-noisy that I am out of phase with God's voice and vision for me.

As I get quiet and become still, I can hear and see what God's future is for my reality. Psalm 46:10 says, *'Be still and know that I am God.'* My future comes from God's possibilities and potential. I pop God's qwiffs and my reality is! What an awesome quantum leap!

Creating Protected Places: Is Your Home Protected?

When we understand that matter has memory and that every good or evil action, word, or thought is recorded, it is our responsibility to remove, purge, and release evil memory. I'm also talking about evil memory that came to you through things you inherited. What about evil acts and words that were spoken over you? Or evil artifacts that are in many homes and places? Imagine what evil is recorded in public places, courthouses, jails, even schools, and the stuff in these places!

The Passover in the book of Exodus, chapter 12, is the story of a protected place. The blood of the Passover lamb was not put on the firstborn child. It was not applied to a person. Rather, the blood was put on the side posts and upper door posts of a place. Anoint your home, your office, your car, even public places in the name of Jesus. The Passover was an event where the children of God looked forward to their Messiah and His blood for deliverance and protection. By anointing your places and belongings with oil in the name of Jesus, you can protect them and connect our Savior's timeless blood over your places. What a quantum leap!

Elsewhen Teaching: Where Yesterday Went and Tomorrow Comes From

Elsewhen is the title of my book. This is an interesting word. Elsewhere means over there, or a place out of town, or out there somewhere. Elsewhen is your consciousness out of time here and into God's upper bandwidth of cosmic consciousness. It is to disconnect from things of this realm and become connected to ideas, visions, and input that comes directly from your Savior, Designer, and Creator.

Elsewhen is the experience of knowing without having to learn or push yourself to know. It is to so behold Jesus Himself, that you comprehend the root of wisdom through the Holy Spirit.

You herein have come to understand that there is a non-physical reality from which this universe and everything in it flows. Jesus Himself is causing your body, your spirit, and everything you have to blink into your reality. Light is slowing down and there is upper bandwidth and knowledge through the Holy Spirit. All the things of life and their purpose for you and your assignment are frequencies being spoken by Christ Himself at this very nanosecond.

Matter has memory, and you can change everything that has been recorded by what you observe, by the words you declare, or by the curses you remove and release in the name of Jesus. You can create protected places by anointing with oil and speaking blessings with your words of faith. Where will you start? What quantum leaps have come up in your spirit? You have been given a new elsewhen cosmic consciousness. Pop those God qwiffs and cause upper bandwidth to change your reality."[12]

---

[12] Van Koevering, David. *Keys to Taking Your Quantum Leap*. Cleveland, TN: Elsewhen Research, 2010. Print

the worship studio

For more information on the ministry of The Worship Studio, please visit our website at:

http://www.theworshipstudio.org

To invite Matt Tommey to speak at you church, conference or event, please contact us at matt@theworshipstudio.org

Conferences Sponsored By The Worship Studio

Each year, The Worship Studio sponsors events to encourage and equip artists to fulfill their creative calling in the Kingdom.

Gathering of Artisans Weekend

Our annual conference focused on releasing the Kingdom through creative expression. Hands-On workshops in Fine Art, Fine Craft, Performing Arts & Media led by master artists. The last weekend of September in Black Mountain, NC outside Asheville, NC.

http://www.gatheringofartisans.com

Unlocking the Heart of the Artist Weekend

An annual retreat in Black Mountain, NC focused on healing and wholeness for artists.

http://www.theworshipstudio.org/unlocking

Unleashing the Creativity of Heaven Weekend

A weekend experience held in your city led by Matt Tommey and master artists from The Worship Studio. It's a great opportunity to gather artists in your church or region for equipping and encouragement.

http://www.theworshipstudio.org/unleashing

For Further Reading on Kingdom Creativity

Sound of Heaven, Symphony of Earth by Ray Hughes

The Lost Glory by Dave Markee

Keys to Taking Your Quantum Leap by David Van Koevering

Finding Divine Inspiration by J. Scott McElroy

Imagine That by Manuel Luz

The Artist's Way by Julia Cameron

www.simply-worship.org by Cathy Little

The Effect of Trauma and How to Deal With It by Jim Banks

Made in the USA
Charleston, SC
15 October 2016